BERE REGIS
PAST AND PRESENT

Hardy's Kingsbere

JOHN PITFIELD and RODNEY LEGG

HALSGROVE

First published in Great Britain in 2006

British Library Cataloguing-in-Publication Data.
A CIP record for this title is available from the British Library.

ISBN 1 84114 554 8
ISBN 978 1 84114 554 9

HALSGROVE

Halsgrove House
Lower Moor Way
Tiverton, Devon EX16 6SS
Tel: 01884 243242
Fax: 01884 243325
Email: sales@halsgrove.com
Website: www.halsgrove.com

Printed and bound in Great Britain by CPI Bath

Frontispiece image: *Bere Regis School open day, mid-1950s.*

Opposite page: *West Street, Bere Regis, in the 1950s.*

CONTENTS

Bere Regis School class photo of 1970. Left to right, back row: Stephen Cox, Janice Day, Amanda Watts, Sonia Ives, Anjeli Keen, Steven Ballet, Robert Presslee, Steven Ives, Kevin Hewitt; third row: Gregory Jones, Martin Runyard, Elaine Elford, Tina Fancy, Beverley Maidment, Sara Booth, Trudy White, Lyndsey McLeod, Susan Austin, Marian Crocker; second row: Sharon Beeden, Lesley Poore, ?, Elizabeth Miller, Mr Stacey (headmaster), Gerald Holloway, Kevin Spicer, Graham Pashen, Christopher Booth; sitting: Timothy Maunder, John Pitfield, John Elford, Kevin Hewitt.

Above: *Bere Regis School class photo, 1950s.*

Bere Regis School sports day c1967 with Donovan Keen winning the 100 yards.

Right: *Mr Arthur Janes outside his saddlery shop, c.1948.*

Watercress workers at the Doddings beds, c.1960.

Farm workers break for lunch near Woodbury Hill, late 1950s.

Acknowledgements

Special thanks are due to many people, but especially to those listed below alphabetically:

Mr S. Bailey	for Woodbury Hill Fair research
Mr A. Bates	for the use of photographs
Bedford & Jesty	for the use of photographs
Mr M. Bennett	for the loan of photographs
Mr and Mrs P. Bennett	for the loan of photos and raising the profile of village history in 2004
Mr G.W. Booth	for use of photographs
Mr M. Eastment	for the loan of photographs
Mr J. England	for help on Bere Regis Scout Hut details
Mr G. Griffin	for permission to use J.W. Boswell's photographs
Mr and Mrs D. Herring	for photographs and material about the church
Mr J. Loxton	for use of material on the Bere Regis website
Mr and Mrs J. Shave	for encouragement and helping me get into places for photography
Mr I. Ventham	for use of photographs
Revd I. Woodward	for church and garden party access
Mr F.P. Pitfield	for allowing me to use his village research with reckless abandon – thanks Dad!

Publishers of local newspapers, in particular the *Western Gazette* and the *Bournemouth Echo*

Ready-Reckoner

For those totally unfamiliar with units and the division of money in the past, here are a few pointers related to passages in the text:

One Shilling (1s.)	one twentieth of a pound sterling
One penny (1d.)	one twelfth of a shilling (i.e. $\frac{1}{240}$th of a pound sterling)
One bushel	dry measure of eight gallons
One foot (1ft)	twelve inches (1 metre = 39.37 inches)
One pound (weight 1lb)	0.453 kg (1kg = 2.2046lb)
Plumber	man who works with lead

Mrs Deakin and Fred Cleall with one of his horses – one of a pair named Colonel and Punch.

INTRODUCTION

In April 2006 a Neolithic hand tool was found on the slopes of Barrow Hill in Bere Regis, Dorset. That find, by my father, influenced my decision to make this book a chronology of events of the area and neatly brings the book, in a circle, to the earliest entry. The Neolithic long barrow on Bere Down was the finest example in this part of the country, before it was destroyed in 1970. People have been living in this place that we now call Bere Regis for over 4,500 years – further evidenced by the even earlier Palaeolithic axe head found at Gallows Hill in 1939.

The name Bere or Beer or Beere or Beare has its origins in many theories and each one is detailed in the time-line of this book. The Regis part is much easier to decide upon. Perhaps in the future it will be spelt differently again, for it was only a few years ago that I received a letter addressed to Bare Regions.

The parish is a large one and extends over an area dominated by chalkland, this being subsumed in the south, under a sandy layer which is denoted by the Heath. The river valley has eroded down to the chalk layer on its path to Wareham six miles away. Two rivers enter the parish, the Bere River from the north-west and the River Piddle from the west, joining on the Heath.

Often described by outsiders as a sleepy little town where nothing much happens and is now bypassed, the village has been the centre of many exciting events. These include King John using the manor-house as the repository for £20,000 in cash, the equivalent of over £10 billion today. Some years later the church had a spire. The church burned down in 1485. Not forgetting that this is one of only a few parishes that have produced an Archbishop of Canterbury. The Civil War resulted in incendiary action at Bere when Parliamentarians burned down the Turberville house at Court Green. Turberville's men rode off to set fire to the nearest Parliamentarian house in revenge. The village was rocked by an earthquake in 1889, fortunately a forgettable one. In the twentieth century the village was the centre of both the country's biggest watercress firm and the biggest independent coach firm in the country. Not to be forgotten in the twentieth century, the church was struck by lightning in 1976 sending one of the 5-ton pinnacles to the ground.

The Turberville family which brought King John to Bere in the early-thirteenth century dominated the village for 500 years with their own kind of logic. As one example: they boasted of their wealth to gain royal favours yet blocked up their fireplaces as a tax evasion ruse. From the mid-seventeenth century and probably long before, they left a legacy of bastard children; this being the basic idea behind Thomas Hardy's *Tess of the d'Urbervilles*. Names that sound a little like Turberville appear in parish records since that time. This book is the first place where a reconstruction of the Turberville manor-house has been presented, helped mainly by a resistivity survey conducted in 2003–04. It is now clear that the complex of buildings was indeed the Palace of King John. For good measure I have reconstructed the brewery just east of the church, which was at its height in Victorian times. Also included is an impression of how the church may have looked, with its spire, by about 1360.

The answer to the obvious question; what is the oldest existing building in the village? Apart from the church, that is Honeycombe Cottage at Shitterton, of which parts date from around the 1580s.

In the seventeenth and eighteenth centuries the people of Bere Regis either had a sense of humour or lacked imagination. The parish records include baptisms of William Williams, Joseph Joseph, Stephen Stephens, Thomas Thomas and Sansom Sansome. Unusual girls' names also appearing were Fortune, Repentance, Prudence, Bathsheba, Patience, Unity and Charity. The boys didn't fare much better, with Penticost, Azarius and Hercules appearing. Also found was one Thomas Hardy (1595) and a Francis Drake (1607).

Original, contemporary, spellings have been retained throughout to illustrate how these have evolved for village areas and names over the centuries.

John Pitfield and Rodney Legg, 2006

Chapter 1

Early Settlement, 3500BC–AD1000

Early Signs of Life in Bere

3500BC: Long Barrow on Bere Down

Dating from between 3500BC and 3000BC in the Neolithic period, the chambered long barrow on Bere Down was the earliest known burial mound in the area, and had been scheduled as an ancient monument. It stood at Ordnance Survey grid reference SY 8298 9725 and was aligned from east to west, being 180ft long and 60ft wide with parallel sides but no sign of the ditches which probably flanked each side, although there was a slight terrace to the south. The mound varied in height, from 8ft high at the east end, which would have covered inhumation burials, to 6ft high at the west end. In between there were five medium-sized brownish sarsen stones, protruding from the middle of the chalk-built barrow, which indicated the presence inside of a burial chamber. None of the boulders was more than 3ft long. The entire south-western side of the mound had been damaged for removal of chalk, perhaps in antiquity for the making of adjacent Iron Age and Romano-British lynchets and field boundaries, and the mound was ploughed to the edge, being at the centre of a modern grain field. This was a Dorset rarity. The closest more or less intact chambered long barrow is the Grey Mare and her Colts above Abbotsbury. The Bere Down barrow was also unusual, compared with the nearest cluster of earthen mounds – with wooden rather than stone chambers – on Cranborne Chase in that it was not placed in silhouette on a hilltop but lay in a downland dip. This record is in the past tense as the mound is completely gone, having been levelled by a bulldozer in about 1970. Although Rodney Legg reported its destruction both to Dorset County Museum and Miss Joyce Melhuish, the chief civil servant responsible for its preservation, no legal action was taken as the matter was judged to be 'out of time'.

3500BC: Neolithic Finds in the Parish

There have been a number of finds dating from the Neolithic period (5,000–2,400 years BC). These include an axe-head of greenstone which was found in the river at Bere in 1896 then a polished flint hand-axe found at Bere Heath Farm in 1907. In 1951 a late-Neolithic flint hand-axe was found near Philliols Farm.

Above: *Bronze Age barrow on Bere Down c.1950. One of the finest in the parish of Bere Regis., it is 85ft (26m) in diameter and 6ft (1.8m) high and near the Roman Road.*

Above: *Neolithic, chambered, long barrow on Bere Down photographed in about 1950. It was one of the finest examples in southern England and was 180ft long and 60ft wide. The height varied from 6–8ft but it was destroyed in 1970.*

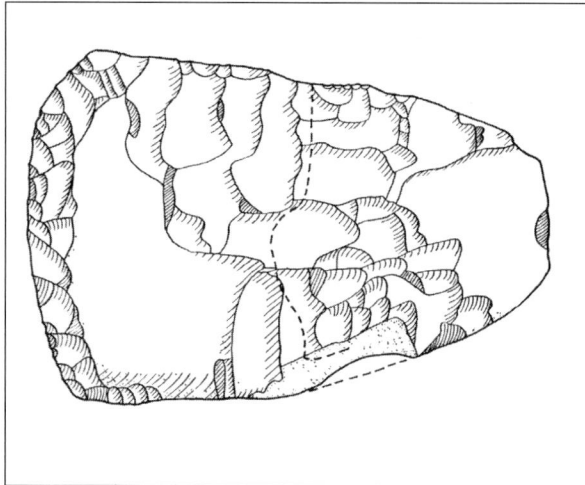

Above: *This Paleolithic hand axe was found at Bere Regis in 1939.*

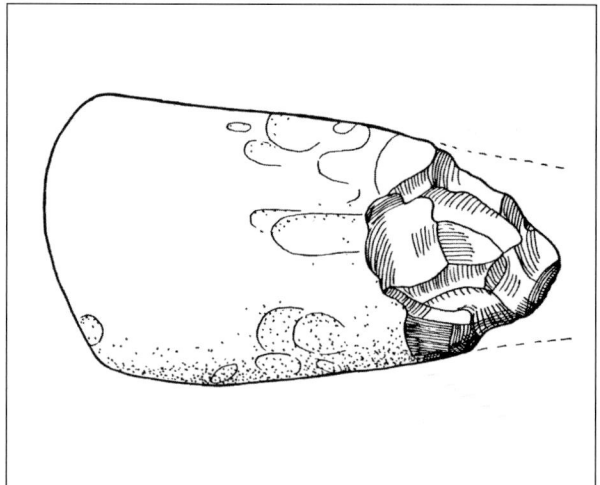

Above: *Neolithic flint axe head found at Bere Heath Farm in 1907.*

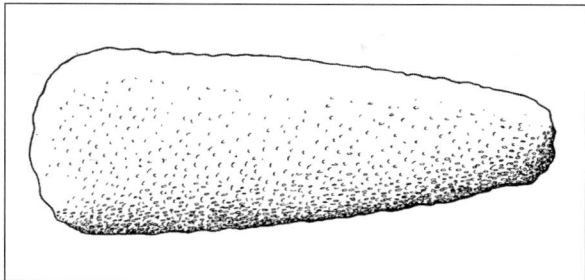

Above: *Neolithic stone axe head found in the river in 1896.*

Right: *This 13ins (33cm) bronze dagger, with bone handle, found in 1840 in a barrow on Roke Down, dates from the Bronze Age.*

Below left: *Bronze Age burial urn found in a barrow on Roke Down on 28 June 1849. The urn is 10.5ins high.*

Below: *Found in August 1845 in a barrow on Roke Down, this burial urn is 11.5ins high.*

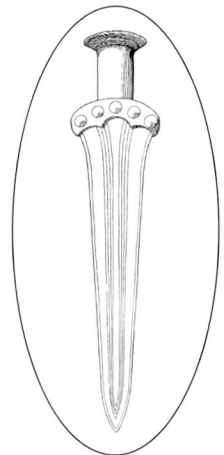

Bronze-Age Finds in the Parish, 2100BC–800BC

2100BC: Bronze Age Barrows

Bronze Age round barrows have fared better, but there were many more of them, with the finest for contents, size and occasional sophistication in shape dating from the Wessex Culture of 2100BC to 1500BC which coincide with the construction of Stonehenge in its final form. There are 50 barrows in Bere Regis parish, from extensive groups on the northern chalk to a scattering of turf-built mounds on the sandy heaths. Prominent and significant mounds have interesting names, such as Hundred Barrow on the 200ft contour of Rye Hill, which may well have been the meeting place for the Anglo-Saxon 'hundred' administrators for the area. Other barrows with names include End Barrow, Fox Barrow, Stand Barrow and Yon Barrow (Yarn Barrow in 1777). Barrow Hill, on the other hand, has been dismissed by field archaeologists as a natural-shaped hill though it may have been named for a burial mound on the top. On the death of antiquarian collector Henry Durden in 1892, his Bronze Age burial urns from excavated Bere Regis barrows were transferred to the British Museum.

As well as finds from excavations of Bronze Age barrows at Bere Regis, there have been two axe-head finds. One was found while the cress beds were being dug at Hollow Oak in 1898, and another found at Muddox Barrow Farm (Skippets) in 1900.

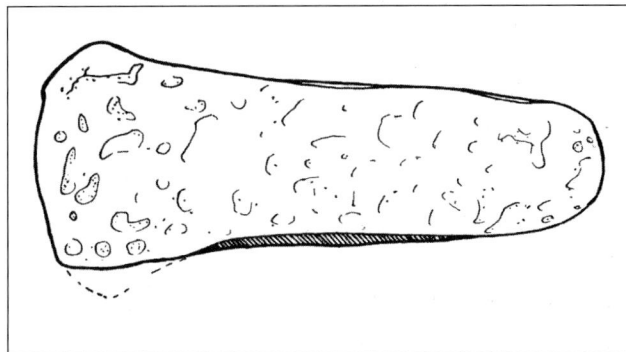

Above: Bronze Age axe head found in about 1900 at Muddox Barrow Farm.

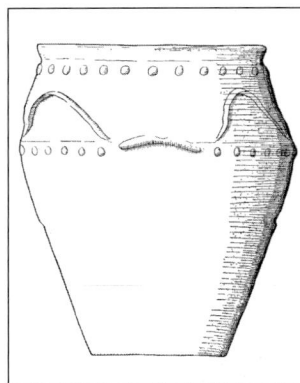

Left: Bronze Age burial urn found in a barrow on Roke Down on 7 July 1845.

Right: Bronze Age burial urn found on 17 October 1846 in a Roke barrow.

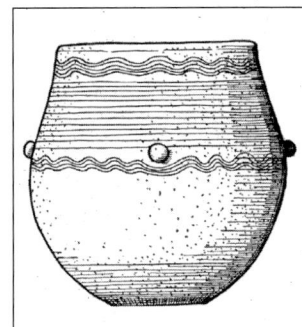

2000BC: Devil's Stone

The Devil's Stone is a contorted sarsen boulder, about 5ft high, that stands on Black Hill, on a slight bank amongst the gorse and heather beside the old road over the heath from Bere Regis to Turners Puddle. It has certainly been there a long time because as with two nearby Bronze Age round barrows – a third of a mile south-east and a similar distance north-west – it was utilised by the Saxons as a convenient marker on wild moorland for setting the boundary between the parishes of Bere and Turners Puddle. Almost certainly the Devil's Stone was erected here in Bronze Age times for some purpose connected with the three round barrow burial mounds that lie in a line along the Damer Hill spur of Black Hill. The stone has smoothed indentations and a kneeling person can fit comfortably into its folds. There is also a depression at the top that might have received votive offerings. Possibly this is pure fancy, but ancient rituals were probably rather bizarre and interesting.

1200BC: Ditches and Banks

Late Bronze Age times, during which emmer and

Right: The Devil's Stone on Black Hill dates from about 2000BC and serves as a marker.

Bere Regis Barrow No. 43 on Bere Heath, near Yearlings' Bottom, seen here in 1969. Called End Barrow, its height is 8ft (2.44m), diameter 66ft (20m). A stray German bomb in 1940 narrowly missed this Bronze Age barrow.

spelt wheat continued to be produced in quantity and had to be separated from cattle-grazing areas by ranch boundaries, linear dykes appeared across both downs and heaths. These can be vaguely dated to between 1500BC and 800BC but may have continued in use into the Iron Age. Examples on either side of Bere Regis are that which were later chosen for the parish boundary, with Milborne St Andrew. The boundary goes down and across the dry valley towards Roke, and to the south are Battery Bank and similar earthworks from Stoke Heath to Wareham Common. Beyond, around Wareham, this seems to have been the ancient forerunner of the northern section of the Anglo-Saxon Town Walls which date from the time of King Alfred the Great and the *Burghal Hidage* against Danish raiders, which was reinforced by Ethelred the Unready or Cnut, and was the third largest in the kingdom. Poole Harbour also had important ports in Iron Age times, at Cleavel Point and Hamworthy, and Bere then and onwards was part of the coastal hinterland.

Celtic Influences

425BC: Woodbury Hill
Celts first crossed the Channel to colonise the British Isles in 450BC. To the east of the present village is Woodbury Hill, a fortified position which contained a small village of its own. It is certain that the surrounding areas were used for agriculture to support the population and the liberal power system then in place. It is now widely accepted that Celtic civilisation was much more sophisticated than we were taught only a generation ago, and the invasion by the Roman Empire of Gaul and later Britain was perpe-

trated to seize precious metals and resources such as gold, evident in the fact that gold Roman coins only appeared after the Celtic lands were invaded. The nearest source of gold in the area was on the fringes of Salisbury Plain. The main 'street' on Woodbury Hill ran north–south with a junction in the middle extending to the west rampart. Farm buildings still stand at this central area.

400BC: Celtic Fields
There are faint remains of Iron Age and Romano-British fields, collectively known as Celtic fields, from Bere Down to Bere Wood but these chalklands have been under cultivation for so long that most traces have been lost. The open arable fields were divided into parcels of land called furlongs. Where the land was sloping there were irregular furrows or platforms called butts, while a triangular piece of land was called a gore. The substantial survival from this period, on Woodbury Hill, is an early Iron Age hillfort, dating from about 400BC. Enclosed by a ditch and bank, it comprises 13 acres of chalk-topped plateau, at 360ft above sea level. This hill rises abruptly from the Bere Stream, with the earthwork beginning near the summit, plus an intermittent though chunky counter-scarp bank which is 25ft wide. Inside, the ditch is 30ft wide and 5ft deep, rising into an inner bank 35–40ft wide and up to 19ft in height. The original entrance, still in use, faces south-west down into the lane across the hilltop. Another entrance, in the north-east corner, carries a public path into Bere Wood. Other openings probably originated later.

331BC: Harvesting
According to a report by a traveller from the Greek colony of Massilia (Marseilles), the south of England was extensively wheat harvested with threshing in the shelter of great barns.

The Romans and Beyond

54BC: Caesar's Influence
Julius Caesar made an expedition to Britain in 54BC and during his reconnaissance opened the south of England to some Roman influence. In 45BC Caesar introduced the 'Julian Calendar' of 365¼ days with the first day of the year being 1 January. This was the result of consultations with the Greek astronomer Sosigenes of Alexandria. Despite the logic of utilising the Earth's movements for the calendar, the church insisted on an Easter-to-Easter year through the middle ages.

Above: *Celtic base-silver stater of 50–60BC found at Bere Regis in the 1980s. The four-horse chariot design is based on Greek symbols.*

Carved Sarmatian horseman of AD175, found in 1985.

AD43: Invasion Roman Style

Britain was invaded by 40,000 Roman troops under Claudius. What is now London was established in the same year, while the push westward included the victory over the Celts at Maiden Castle, south-west of what is now Dorchester, in AD44. This means that the Romans would have passed through Bere at about this time, probably brushing aside any resistance. A Roman garrison was established at Woodbury Hill. A Roman coin of Septimus Severus (AD193–211) was found in 1960 at a depth of 3ft in the west bank of Woodbury Hill during the digging of a pipe trench by Mr Lake.

AD100: Bagwood Settlement

The Romano-British settlement at Bagwood and its adjoining preserved agger or causeway of Roman road – about 270ft of which survives – are just inside the parish of Bere Regis, though they lie on the side and top of the hill overlooking Winterborne Kingston. Immediately north-west of the section of road, on the summit, was a Roman well which was excavated by the antiquary Charles Warne in 1870. Another well was discovered and explored by Geoffrey Toms in 1962. He went down it to 70ft and found coins dating from AD98–273, as well as a wide range of animal bones, broken quern stones and pottery. On the ground, he followed the settlement across 5 acres, which were strewn with evidence of intensive use over several centuries until about AD350.

European Influences

AD175: Sarmation Carving Find

Building work on former barns in the village in 1985 led to a Purbeck marble carving of a Sarmatian horseman being found in a skip. These tribesmen, from what is now eastern Poland, wore distinctive beehive-shaped helmets. The stone was damaged, and had therefore probably been discarded as no longer being of commercial quality, having been intended as a memorial stone for a grave to a Roman auxiliary at Ribchester or some other garrison on the approaches to Hadrian's Wall. Some 8,000 defeated Sarmatian horsemen, who had fought effectively against the Romans in the Dacian wars, were drafted into their captors' army in AD175. Marcus Aurelius sent 5,500 of them to Britain, to support hard-pressed legions in the province of Britannia. The obvious advantage of having them stationed in Lancashire was that they would be unable to march home.

AD407: Dark Age Summary

The Romans withdrew from the British Isles as they were needed to defend Rome against the 'barbarians'. For the first time in 360 years Britain had to adopt to native rule. Saxon settlers arrived in AD441 while the

Typical Romano-British pottery find in Bere Regis. The hard sandy clay is evident in the break lines.

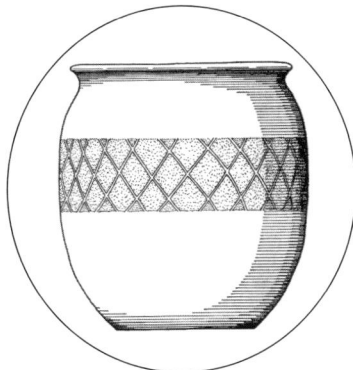

Pottery vessel found at Bagwood excavation.

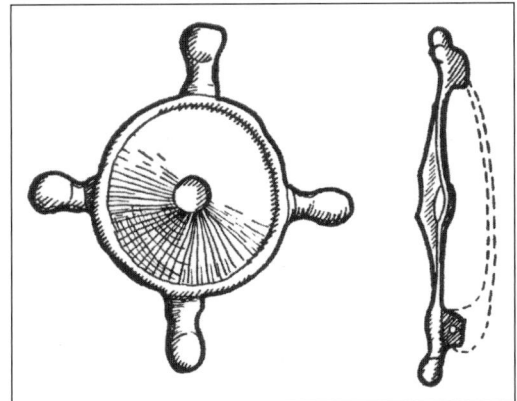

Brooch found during excavation of Bagwood Coppice site.

Britons made a last appeal to Rome for help in defence against the invaders. However Honorius told them to defend themselves. By AD449 both Saxons and Angles were arriving in Britain and Roman influence can be accepted as having ceased by AD491. The Great Plague of Justinian reached Britain in AD547 but after this the invaders and the Britons set about warring and in AD577 three British Kings, Coinmail, Condidan and Farinmail were killed. The Battle of Adam's Grave near Alton Priors (in AD591) resulted in Ceol ('Old King Cole') becoming King of Wessex.

The kingdoms of Kent, Northumbria, East Anglia and Mercia fought amongst themselves in a most fierce and bloody way until AD787 when the first Viking raiders invaded Britain. Viking raids began in earnest from AD793 when they sacked the church on Lindisfarne, then the monastery at Jarrow. Fighting continued amongst the British kingdoms with periodic battles with Vikings who had made ground in Scotland and Ireland in AD794 and AD795. The Kingdom of Wessex, which covered more than half of the British Isles, became the dominant force, even able to repel a Viking attack on Southampton in AD840.

Ethelred, King of Wessex, had varying success against Danish invaders during AD871 but died of his wounds and was succeeded by King Alfred of Wessex. The Danes attacked Alfred in AD878 but he escaped, rallied support and defeated them at the Battle of Edington. The following year, AD879, King Alfred had to cede the north of Britain to Guthrum the Danish leader under the Treaty of Wedmore and by AD890 King Alfred was instituting the power of the King's Court while founding a regular army and navy. Just in time; in AD892 a Viking invasion fleet of 330 ships landed with such confidence that they had brought their wives and children in a clear attempt to settle. Alfred's son Edward engaged the enemy at Farnham and pushed them back to Thorney Island in AD893. King Alfred and Edward finished them off in AD896 having pushed them further back and into Essex.

Alfred the Great of Wessex died on 26 October AD899 and was succeeded by his son, Edward the Elder, King of Wessex, and titled himself 'King of the Angles and Saxons'. Edward, then his son Athelstan, and his son Edmund continued to do battle with invaders until in AD946 Edmund's son Edred's forces murdered Eric Bloodaxe, leader of the Danes, at York in AD954. King Edred then ruled all of England. Through Edwig and Edgar, 12-year-old King Edward (the Martyr) became King in AD975 only to be murdered at Corfe Castle on 18 March AD978 by his step-mother who fled to Bere Regis.

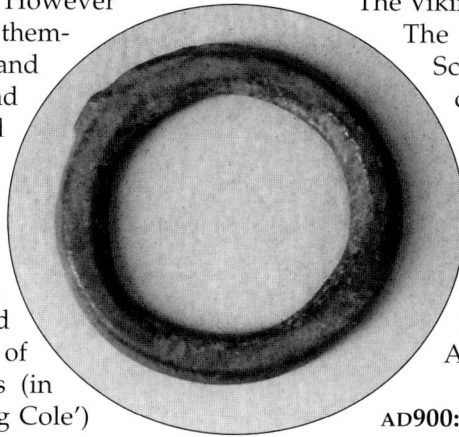

This cast bronze ring, probably to secure a thin leather strap or belt, was found north of Bere Regis in 1993.

AD787: Viking Bere

The Vikings made their first raids on Britain. The name 'Bere' is a word of Scandinavian origin signifying a cluster of buildings or a farmstead. Its old form was *byr*, the same as the Icelandic *boor*, a farm, which still survives in the 'cow-byres' of Scotland and the northern counties of England. Settlement of Bere can be considered an entity at England's unification under King Alfred.

AD900: Saxon Bere

Bere in Dorset, as a name, dates from Saxon times and possibly derives from the Old English *bearu* ('grove') according to the Oxford Dictionary of English Place-names. Bere, however, is a widespread place-name that can come from several other roots, such as *bere* ('barley'), *baer* ('pasture') and burh ('borough').

'Regis', for royal ownership, was added later to the Dorset Bere, to distinguish it from Beres or Beers elsewhere. Beer places in Devon are thought to derive from *bearu* ('grove' as in our Bere) whereas Beers in Dorset and Somerset (such as Beer Hackett) are believed to have their origins in *baer* ('pasture'). Simple sounding place-names are often the hardest to decipher.

AD978: A Queen's Bolt Hole

King Edward the Martyr, having just returned from a hunting expedition, called at the Royal House at Corfe to visit his step-mother Queen Elfrida, on 18 March AD978. He was greeted at the gate, while still on horseback, with a cup of wine. During this distraction another person stabbed him fatally. His alarmed horse bolted and with Edward's foot caught in a stirrup dragged him some way. The King was soon dead and his body was hidden in a nearby cottage before being buried in a humble grave at Wareham. His remains were later taken in great state to Shaftesbury Abbey for reburial. Immediately after the assassination Queen Elfrida fled to the Royal House at Bere with her own son Ethelred.

These events were recorded in Bishop Asser's *Life of Alfred* and represent the first mention of Bere in a document. Ethelred reportedly wept over the killing of his 15-year old half-brother Edward and was punished by the Queen.

There were no whips in the house where the Queen and her son stayed. She seized a bundle of wax candles and with that Ethelred was flogged. Yet he remembered the days at Bere and the fury of Elfrida. Ever after he hated wax candles and would have none burnt before him all the days of his life.

Impression of the royal house at Bere Regis at the time that Queen Elfrida fled to Bere Regis from Corfe in AD978. Its position was probably near the road, where the tithe barn replaced it and was fitted out with rooms and comfortable facilities.

Elfrida was the real power at this time but Ethelred was King from AD978–1016.

1000: Paying the Danes

At the time of King Ethelred and until 1084 most of England was subject to an annual tax called Danegeld or the Geld Tax, payable to the invading Danish, and was essentially a payment of 'blackmail' not to invade further into the country. There were many manors in Dorset and these were each divided into 39 Hundreds of about 100 hides. A hide was determined as being an area of land sufficient to employ a team of oxen and amounted to about 120 acres (48 hectares). It took the invading Normans 20 years to put a stop to those payments and arrange their own taxes, which adopted the same systems of assessment.

Clockwise from top left (in date order):

Excavations in August 1963 found original Norman footings for the chancel of the church.

The beautifully carved font in the church dates from 1130.

Carved royal head in Bere Regis church, said to represent King John, although it could be earlier, possibly King Stephen.

Mediaeval belt buckel of the thirteenth or fourteenth century with gold-punched decoration. It was found where Butt Lane crosses Bere Down in May 1990.

Chapter 2

The Middle Ages

Invasion

1066: Norman Invasion

Amongst the invading force that followed William, Duke of Normandy, on 28 September 1066 was one Payne de Turberville. Turberville was instrumental in helping William conquer the Saxons at Glamorganshire, and for this he received a knighthood and the lordship and castle of Coity in Wales. Other branches of the family established themselves in Warwickshire, Wiltshire and Berkshire early in the thirteenth century. It is probable that the John de Turberville of Bere was from the Wiltshire branch of the family. He had been commissioned by King John from 1199 to find hunting grounds and appropriate houses to use on his trips around the country. There was already a manor-house at Bere Regis near the river below the church, in the hands of royalty.

John de Turberville's first mention in connection with Bere was in 1202 when he was involved in surveying the house then rebuilding and enlarging it for planned visits by King John starting in 1204. Huge sums of money were spent on the house and grounds to make it a base for hunting trips in the surrounding forests and fields. After King John's death in 1216, John de Turberville apparently took over the manor-house on Court Green for himself and his family.

1066: Pre-invasion Bere

At the time of the conquest in 1066 the tenants of the areas in and around Bere were as follows: the royal manor was an individual manor held 'in lordship' by Edward the Confessor. Shitterton consisted of 5 hides, was held by Mr Ulviet and was worth 100 shillings per year. The Church held lands of one hide and 20 acres and the priest was Revd Bristuard. Doddingsbere Farm had an area of half a hide and had a water-mill. It was worth 20 shillings a year and was held by Mr Leomer. Turnerspiddle covered 6 hides and was held by Mr Gerling. Bryanspiddle was held by Mr Azor and covered 5 hides. There were two parts of Milborne Stileham included in Bere Hundred. The first was of 2 hides and was held by Mr Dodo. The second part was held by Mr Swain.

1086: Post-invasion Bere

At the time of the Domesday Survey the 'Hidage of Bera Hundred' was valued in total at £30.12s.5d but the royal manor was now held in lordship by King William. Hugh Fitz Grip probably had use of the manor-house, but was based in Wareham tenanting farms across a wide area with other family members. The church and lands were still under the stewardship of the priest Bristuard, but Hugh Fitz Grip held Shitterton (then called Scetra or Scetre) and was worth 120 shillings a year. The wife of Hugh Fitz Grip held Doddingsbere, which was worth 50 shillings a year. It was sub-leased to William de Monasteriis. 'Turnerspiddle' was also held by the wife of Hugh Fitz Grip and sub-tenanted to William Tonitruus. Bryanspiddle, of 5 hides, was held by the Revd Godric. Milborne Stileham was still in two parts, the first was tenanted by Odo Fitz Eurebold and the second part was still held by the Swain family, although the tenant farmer was Mr Osmund.

1130: Oldest Object Still in Use

This date is carved on the font in the church and is the oldest object in that building. It was obviously installed when the church was much smaller, and built of stone and timber.

King John, 1165–1216

1140: King John or King Stephen

At this time the columns in the church, being Transitional Norman and of short cylindrical shape with square abaci, were built into the church. This allowed the addition of aisles on both the north and the south. A crowned head carved on one of these columns, together with other grotesque faces, is locally taken to be the face of King John. However, it is almost certainly that of a real person – possibly King Stephen, whose troubled reign was full of such strained looks.

1150: Origins of the Fair

Probably by about 1150 Woodbury Hill Fair had its small beginnings. Local custom has it that a travelling cloth salesman spread out his wares to dry after being caught in a storm. Some passers-by assumed they were for sale and each year after this he repeated his good fortune. Others quickly joined in.

1202: Manor-House Improvements

From 1202 to 1203 the Royal House at Bere was improved to be fit for visits by King John (1199–1216) on his trips around the country for hunting and to satisfy his keenness of travelling. The house had been in existence, at what is now Court Green, for over 200 years and used by various landed administrating families. King John's trips included his entourage of many courtiers, scribes and papers, as well as security guards for his money. The renovation work was supervised by the 'viewer' (surveyor) John de Turberville and a total of £47.13s.2d was spent.

1203: Further Manor-House Work

During 1203 and 1204 more work was carried out at the royal house at Bere. This was under the supervision of viewers Elijah de Bere and Gilbert Calve who were probably brought in to bring the standards up to royal approval. A total of £56.17s.7d was spent bringing the total to £104.10s.9d – almost a quarter of a million pounds in today's money. The complex built at this time was located near where the building that remains on this site, with the old house being converted to a tithe barn. King John made his first visit to Bere on 27–29 June 1204.

1204: King John's Favourite Palace

King John seems to have regarded Bere Regis as one of his favourite palaces, being more than a mere hunting lodge. It was more intimate in scale than Clarendon Palace, near Salisbury. He came to Bere Regis, with his closest coteries, at least once during most of the years when he was in England, rather than preoccupied with his French possessions. These visits are well documented. In 1835 the archivist at the Tower of London, Sir Thomas Duffus Hardy (1804–78), edited the Patent Rolls of John's reign and compiled from them an itinerary which places the King at his lodge in Bere in Dorset between Purbeck and Cranborne Chase. Contemporary hunting lodges in and around Dorset include King John's House at Tollard Royal, in the heart of Cranborne Chase, King John's Palace at Motcombe in Gillingham Forest, and Creechbarrow Lodge in the Isle of Purbeck. Of that trio, the Creech building – footings of which survive on the 634ft summit of Creech Barrow Hill – was a lookout rather than a palace. It is shown on Ralph Treswell's Purbeck map of 1575 as a tower with a door and two windows above, perched on the conical-shaped hill with a herd of deer being represented ranging across the wilderness between it and 'Stowboro' (Stoborough). Similar wild countryside lay on the other side of the River Frome between Wareham and Bere Regis. Woodbury Hill is visible from Creech Barrow.

1205: Three Royal Visits

Improvements to the palace at Court Green included the spending of £7.17s.4d, then later £8.13s.10d., over a period of several weeks for work on the house, mews and smithy. It is thought that a stable block was built on the back of the tithe barn and the surrounding gardens were in place by this time. King John made three visits to Bere in 1205. These were 7–8 January, 25–27 June and 18–21 August. He placed an order for five barrels of wine on 13 January to be brought from Southampton to re-stock the residence.

1205: No War; Holiday at Bere

One of King John's visits to Bere Regis came after landing at Studland on the abandonment of the proposed invasion of Normandy. He wrote a letter dated 25 May in a very unusual fit of piety ordering his bailiff to cause a fair crucifix to be set up 'in our chapel at Bere' [attached to the home].

1205: King John's Expenses

On King John's orders 13s.4d. was paid for the keep of the sick horse of Randolf Parmentarius and its attendant at Bere. He was a tailor to the King and very important during the King's visits. Five doliums of wine were ordered to be sent to Bere on 25 October, for which Alexander of Wareham was paid, together with supplying the King's houses at Dorchester as well.

1206: Christmas for a King

King John made two visits to Bere Regis, on 5–7 January and 13–14 December. The cross ordered by King John is placed in the church on the instructions given to the bailiff, and is described as 'handsome'. Wine to be sent from Southampton included one barrel to Bere, ordered 18 February as replenishment. While at Bere on 13 December, King John was preparing for Christmas, which he would spend at Winchester. His order to the Sheriff of Southampton, to be sent to Winchester was 1,500 fowls, 5,000 eggs, 20 oxen, 100 pigs and 100 sheep.

1207: Simon de Montfort

In February, King John seized the English estates of Simon de Montfort, including that at Bere Regis, ostensibly for recovery of a debt. The properties were restored again in March 1207, but confiscated again before the end of the same year and granted to Henry's brother Edmund. Simon de Montfort also had estates in France and returned there, changing sides to support Pope Innocent III against King John. One of the conditions of a reconciliation between the Pope and King John was that Simon de Montfort's properties were to be returned to de Montfort, which came into effect in 1215, but de Montfort was killed at the siege of Toulouse on 25 June 1218. His third son, also Simon de Montfort (c.1208–1265) petitioned for the return of his family's estates beginning in 1231. A license was granted to 'our trusty and well-beloved Simon of Montfort' by King Henry III in June 1232 to:

... keep in his own hands or bestow at his will any escheats of land held by Normans of his fee in England, which may hereafter fall in, until our lands of England and Normandy shall be one again.

Although unpopular with both Church and state, Simon consolidated his position by marrying the King's sister Eleanor on 7 January 1238. He got involved with formulating new constitutional laws but was killed at the Battle of Evesham on 4 August 1265.

1207: £20,000 in Cash at Bere
King John proposed a large kitchen be erected at the manor-house at Court Green to satisfy his requirements while at the village. King John exacted a thirteenth of all movables from both clergy and laity throughout the realm. He appointed his manor of Bere as the place of payment of the £20,000 raised, 'paid by the Justiciary FitzPeter into our Chamber at Bere by the hands of Ralph the Chamberlain'. It is suggested that some of this was spent to improve the village church, replacing some of the wooden structure with stone. King John made two visits to Bere Regis. These were on 28 March and 4–5 September.

1207–08: New Kitchen at Manor-House
The bailiff ordered two tons of rushes and sand for re-flooring the manor-house at Bere. On 3 March 1208 the sheriff was ordered to have a kitchen built at Bere, sufficient to cook two or three oxen at the same time. The kitchen was to cost 30s., so was almost certainly a wooden construction

1209: Manor-House Now a Palace
King John made two visits to Bere Regis, on 1 July and 18 September 1209 and by this time much of the manor-house at Court Green had been completed to King John's orders. Accounts reveal that this palace was not simply one building, but a cluster of buildings, surrounded by a wall and perhaps a moat. There was a King's Chamber, chapel, hall, Queen's Chamber, cellar, kitchen, granary and stables. These separate buildings were connected with covered ways, and lighting was furnished by candles or oil-lamps in the King's quarters. Lawns were provided around the palace with a King's garden and a fishpond.

1210–14: King John at Bere
King John made two visits to Bere, the first on 13 January 1210, then again on 3 October 1210. There were none in 1211 or 1212, but in 1213 the visit dates were 26–27 June 1213 and 4–5 July 1213.

1215–16: Two More Royal Visits
King John visited Bere once in 1215, on 4 February. Later that year, on 15 June, he was made to sign the Magna Carta at Runnymeade, forcing him to relinquish control of some land to the barons and limiting the power of the monarchy.

King John's last visit to Bere was on 19–20 June 1216. He died at Newark, aged 38, on 19 October 1216.

The Royal Fair

1216: Charter for Fair
A royal charter was granted for Woodbury Hill Fair, which had grown from nothing during previous years. By the time of the charter it was a thriving concern, probably centred on the 20 September Nativity of the Blessed Virgin Mary, where waters would have been taken at the Anchoret's well, which may have been dedicated to the Blessed Virgin Mary.

1231: More Royal Support for Fair
One of the oldest and largest annual fairs in England was held above Bere Regis, on Woodbury Hill, for more than 750 years. Like several others in Dorset and Wiltshire it utilised for its stockade the redundant earthworks of an Iron Age fort, with other examples being Poundbury Camp and Lambert's Castle to the west and Yarnbury Castle to the north.

Such fairs were invariably located beside ancient highways. That on Woodbury Hill owed its legitimacy to a series of royal charters. Three were granted by Henry III (1231, 1235 and 1266) and confirmed by Edward II in 1325. The fair started with a single trade day, but soon attracted numerous stalls with harvest-time commodities, and attracted farmers and supplies from across much of southern England. 'Kingesbere' as a placename – adapted into 'Kingsbere' by Thomas Hardy – first appears on a charter from 1280.

A Powerful Family and the Growth of Church Affairs

1235: Turbervilles at Manor-House
Around about 1235, or at least during the reign of King Henry III (1216–1272) it was recorded that Sir John Turberville owned the manor-house at Bere. It is almost certain that this was the same John Turberville who did the surveying on the house for King John in 1202.

1255: Ownership Succession Begins
Around 1255, Sir John Turberville's eldest son, Sir Brian Turberville, was in ownership of the manor-house at Court Green, Bere Regis.

1259: De Montfort's Son Returns
In 1259 the manor of Bere Regis was being held by Simon de Montfort, Earl of Leicester, but in consequence of his rebellion, it was granted to the King's brother Edmund. From 1269 half of the manor of Bere Regis passed to the Abbess of Tarrant. Many of the abbesses are buried in the churchyard, with the extension of the south aisle said to be built upon the grave stones of the Abbesses. The last Abbess,

Margaret Russell requested in her will of 1567, to be buried in Bere church.

1274: The Turbervilles and Abbesses

Sir John Turberville was named as being the lord of *[half]* the Hundred of Bere in 1274. He was the eldest son and heir of Sir Brian. He married Ellen (or Elianora).

1293: The Abbess of Tarrant's Lands

In 1293 the Abbess of Tarrant, at Tarrant Crawford, claimed that her manor of *[half]* Bere comprised 'a fair, market, free warren and the whole forest of Bere' and that she held a moiety over these as well as rights to standing timber.

The Boundary Oak in Bere Wood.

1295: End of Borough Status

Representation in Parliament brought an end to the title 'borough' for Bere Regis, which before this had only entitled the village to a chartered fair and a Wednesday market. During the reign of King Edward I (1272–1307), Bere was made a free borough. At this time Bere had a market and the Sheriff of Dorset used to make his proclamations at the market cross. The market-place in Bere was situated at the cross.

1297: Briantspuddle

Brianus de Thorberville (Bryan Turberville – son of Sir John and Isabel?) gave his name to the small hamlet over the River Piddle to the south-west of the village, to be called 'Piddle Turberville' for himself. It was subsequently called 'Bryan's Piddle', before finally becoming Briantspuddle.

1303: Sir John Turberville

By this date and perhaps for a little time before 1303, Sir John Turberville, the eldest son of Sir John Turberville, together with his wife Isabel, were jointly holding land at Bere. This Sir John was paying an annual fine of 4 shillings to King Edward I each Michaelmas for a property infringement by one of his ancestors. The ancestor had enclosed a piece of forest in Bere Wood for his own, when it actually belonged to the Earl of Hereford.

   This Sir John was the Sheriff of Dorset in 1303 and the Sheriff of Somerset in 1304, becoming Knight of the Shire for Dorset in Parliament in 1305. He died in 1309.

1309: Another Sir John Turberville

Sir John Turberville, eldest son and heir of Sir John Turberville (1303) succeeded his father in 1309 as lord of *[half]* the manor of Bere. He had married Joan (or Joanna) and died before 1346.

1327: Parson of Bere

King Edward III's reign between 1327 and 1377 was the period during which the 'parson of Bere' was noted as being Reginald de Stoke at some time.

1346: Sir Richard Turberville

By this date Sir Richard Turberville, Sir John's eldest son and heir, had become lord of the manor of Bere. Sir Richard is referred to in 1346 as holding land in Bere as the successor to his father. In 1362 Sir Richard is also mentioned as being one of two collectors of tenths and fifteenths in Dorset. He married, first, Eleanor, daughter of Sir Thomas Norris, and they had a son, Robert. Sir Richard's second marriage was to Cecilia, sister of John, Lord Beauchamp of Hatch, but not until his daughter, Juliana was born. Sir Richard Turberville died in 1362.

1348: The Black Death

About July the Black Death (*Yersinia pestis*) arrived at Bere Regis, having spread from Melcombe Regis at Weymouth in June. Melcombe Regis was the administrative area along the northern length of Weymouth Harbour and was third, behind London and Bristol, in its contribution of ships towards the siege of Calais. The monk compiling the *Grey Friars' Chronicle* in King's Lynn, Norfolk, recorded:

In this year 1348, in Melcombe in the county of Dorset, a little before the Feast of St John the Baptist [24 June], *two ships, one of them from Bristol, came alongside. One of the sailors had brought with him from Gascony the seeds of the terrible pestilence and, through him, the men of that town of Melcombe were the first in England to be infected.*

Ecclesiastical records show that the disease spread fast and reached its peak across Dorset at the end of the year. New vicars were appointed in Shaftesbury in November and December 1348, and in January and May, 1349. The prior at Wareham died in October 1348. Two new vicars were instituted there in December, with further replacements in the following

May and June. The clergy were particularly vulnerable to infection, as they ministered to the sick and dying, and 100 Dorset parishes needed fresh incumbents over the winter and spring of 1348–49.

Within 18 months this plague had killed over 1.2 million people in Britain representing about a third of the population. It is unlikely that Bere Regis escaped the effects of the Black Death, so probably up to 200 people died by the end of 1349 in the village. Any details of this time were destroyed during the big fire of Bere Regis in 1788, when the parish records were lost.

1350: Boundary Oak

The late Boundary Oak, the ancient oak between Bere Wood and Bloxworth, dated back to long before its first mention in 1350. It provided the wood for backing and binding the service book on the litany desk in Bloxworth parish church. The present name-holder, just inside Kimberley Wood, was planted in 1978 'to replace one believed to date from Domesday, 1087', to quote its cast-iron plaque. The predecessor's hollow remains were left tumbled about, beside the ancient bluebell-covered ditch, which marks the legal line of the boundary.

1360: Church with Spire?

The Gough Map of Great Britain (also known as the Bodleian Map) is the oldest surviving map of Great Britain, dating from around 1360. It had been donated to the Bodleian Library, Oxford, in 1809 by Richard Gough together with his other effects. Little is known about the map except that Richard Gough bought it at a sale in 1774 for half a crown (2s.6d.). The identity of the map maker is unknown, but some

An interpretation of how the church may have looked in 1340.

think that it could be the work of a monk at a monastery, perhaps in Essex. Certain clues suggest that the date would be after 1360, but before 1366.

Careful examination of the part of the map showing Dorset presents some difficulties, but despite many features being completely unfamiliar, there are a number of points which can be readily identified, such as Portland, Poole Harbour, Lulworth Cove, and the towns of Dorchester, Wareham and Christchurch, all showing their abbeys or churches. At a position on the map that could be interpreted as 9 miles (14.5 km) north of Lulworth Cove there is shown a village or town that can only be Bere Regis. The particularly interesting point about the church, shaded in red, as with other towns, is that the church is shown with a spire slightly east of the middle of the building, and about 2.4 times the height of the roof. It has long been thought that Bere church had a tower of some sort just west of the chancel, central to the general layout. The map hardly stands up as conclusive evidence, but many churches are represented as not having spires, and some are without towers at all, so the question is: why show Bere Regis church with a spire on the map?

1362: Sir Robert Turberville

Sir Robert Turberville (1356–1424) succeeded his father as lord of the manor, being his eldest son and heir in 1362 at the age of six. He later married Margaret, daughter of Lord Carew of Bedington. Robert was knighted in 1403, aged 47 and died aged 68 on 6 August 1424.

1405: Arrow Flights at Bere

An order exists from the reign of Henry V for the supply by the shires of a million goose feathers. They were needed for the arrow flights of English and Welsh bowmen. Such orders must have been commonplace, together with those for the making of the 24 arrows in each archer's sheaf. So too would have been commands for practising archery at the butts, and legislation aimed at curbing other pursuits and distractions.

The targets for Bere's bowmen were set up on chalky terraces above the east side of Butt Lane. Proficiency was reached when an archer could discharge ten arrows in a minute, although 20 an hour was a rate of fire that the best bowmen could achieve in the field. English archers won the Battle of Crécy in 1346 with a fire-power that was not to be equalled and exceeded until the American Civil War. Even the famous victory at Agincourt in 1415 did not match the fusillade at Crécy, although both were won with clouds of wood, iron and feathers that blacked out the sun.

1408: Chapel on Woodbury Hill

The Anchoret's Chapel on the western side of the plateau inside the Iron Age earthworks on Woodbury

Hill is of obscure origins. Anchorets had their place in early monasticism. It was a term for those who withdrew from society to live alone. Such recluses, either male or female, were 'immured in a cell, or anchorage, often built near some monastery or church'.

The chaplain on Woodbury Hill at the turn of the fifteenth century, in 1408, was John Spearhauk. He was followed in 1411 by John Hyde. The building was a ruin by the eighteenth century, with footings that were crumbling away, in 1770. The site is now a hump in the grass to the south of the public path which crosses the hill.

Edward VI (1461–83) coin found at Rye Hill in 2003.

The Anchoret's Well on Woodbury Hill, lay 50ft to the south-east of the chapel and a similar distance west from the southern end of the farm buildings inside the earthworks and was exceptionally deep. As with many wells associated with sacred sites, its waters were linked with health cures, and their powers said to be at their greatest on its dedication day, 21 September. This is St Matthew's Day and the autumnal equinox. Pilgrims to Woodbury in the Middle Ages assembled to drink and cleanse themselves in the holy water. The Dean Chandler's register of visitations also notes that the vicar of Bere church was John Belle.

1411: Protestant Heresy

Thomas Turke was the vicar at Bere and is recorded in the Dean Chandler's visitation register. He is said to have 'abjured for heresy' in 1414 when he was tried for Protestant heresy. There were two other cases of suspected 'Lollards' on record.

1420: John Morton

Bere benefited from John Morton's inspired largesse – uplifted both literally and figuratively – as it was directed at providing the parish church with a superb early-Tudor hammer-beam roof to the nave. It is adorned with gilded bosses and coloured life-size figures garbed in contemporary costume. Morton, quite understandably, chose to be buried beneath an effigy in his own cathedral at Canterbury, though the tomb split and its only remaining contents in 1670 comprised the skull, which Archbishop Sheldon was persuaded to present to his brother Ralph.

The chief statesman of the Lancastrian camp during the Wars of the Roses (1455–1487), Cardinal John Morton (1420–1500), Archbishop of Canterbury and Chancellor of England, was born in one of the 'ancient, humble cottages' of Milborne Stileham,

Philliols farmhouse was built in 1906 after the previous building burned down in 1904. Three eighteenth-century farm buildings are to the west of the farmhouse. One barn has the date 1748 in glazed bricks on one end. Previous buildings date back to at least 1460 when John Filoll leased land to another farmer near Doddings. The tenant of Philliols in 1646 was Jeffrey Samways.

where the Mortons long continued to be lords of the manor. Both Bere Regis and Milborne St Andrew are in the frame, specifically and respectively the sites of Court House and the manor-house, which belonged to his father, Richard Morton, who had migrated from Nottinghamshire. It was in the old parish of Milborne Stileham that he grew up. The young John was educated by Benedictine monks at Cerne Abbey, and progressed to Balliol College, Oxford.

1424: William Turberville
William Turberville succeeded his father as lord of the manor at Bere in 1424, being his eldest son and heir. William (1394–1451) married, first, Joan, daughter of Nicholas Toner, and had four sons: John, Richard, Hugh and Robert. His second marriage was to Edith, daughter of John Newburgh and there were three more children; John, Humphrey and Joan. In 1434 he qualified as being gentry, 'named among the gentry of this county who could dispend £10 per annum'. William Turberville died in 1451 and was probably buried in the south aisle of the church where a floor slab, since removed to near the font, had the part of an inscription 'Orate pro a'i'a' Will'i-'.

1451: John Turberville
The lord of the manor of Bere passed to John Turberville in 1451, John being the eldest son of William (1424). John Turberville (1431–c.1490) married Alice, daughter of Hugh Bramshott, but all their children died and he left no heir. By 1485 he was Sheriff of both Dorset and Somerset. Sir John Turberville was a warm supporter of the Lancastrian cause, and was rewarded a month after the victory at Bosworth Field had placed Henry VII on the throne with the offices of Constable of Corfe Castle and Marshal of the Royal Household.

1460: Doddings Mill
A deed dated 26 April is of an indenture whereby John Filoll, esq., leases to Ralph Lavender and John Lavender, his brother, a water-mill in 'Doddyngbyre next Kyngesbyre', and two closes in Doddyngbyre called 'le Fount' and 'Hankeshey' for the life of Ralph at the yearly rent of 5s. and then for the life of John. A condition was that the lessees were to repair the mill.

1485: Cardinal Moreton
Cardinal Moreton had been Archbishop of Canterbury at the end of the fifteenth century and had been at one time rector of the adjoining parish of Bloxworth. Moreton paid for the church roof at Bere Regis. One account says that he had the work executed in his former diocese of Ely and sent down to Bere by sea. Another story, contradicted by the appearance of the carving, was that the roof was made in Rome. The nature of the carving is that it is heavy in design, but coarse in execution, but it is still

the most magnificent tie-beam roof built into such a small town's church. One curious feature is that of a centrally mounted huge head with fat cheeks, which stares down on the centre of the church. The face is attributed to Cardinal Moreton himself.

The face of Cardinal Morton on a roof boss in the church.

Nave roof of the church in about 1925.

1486: Roof Lost in Church Fire
John Morton, who was born in Milborne Stileham and part of the parish of Bere Regis, became Cardinal Morton, the Archbishop of Canterbury in 1486 until his death in 1500 aged 80. His gift to Bere Regis church of the elegantly carved nave roof was almost certainly instigated by a disaster. In the opinion of the builders and architect who carried out the restoration in 1875, the building had been the victim of a 'destructive fire which had calcined the stones of the south arcade and evidently destroyed the greater part of the building'. The first person the church would have turned to was John Turberville who had just been made Sheriff of Dorset and he was closely connected to the Morton family.

1490: Richard Turberville

In about this year, brother and heir of John Turberville, Richard, succeeded to the manor of Bere, being second son of William Turberville (1451). He married Alice on the birth of his daughter, but married again, Joan, daughter of Thomas Benham of Wiltshire, and they had four children; John, Thomas, Richard and Edith. Richard Turberville died in 1505 and was buried in the church. A floor slab, formerly in the south aisle, once bore the inscription: 'Richard Turberville, arm bearer, lord of Bere Regis, and Joan his wife' (translated from the Latin).

1500: Cardinal Moreton's Legacy

The nave roof in the church at Bere Regis was paid for by Cardinal Morton and completed in about 1488. He gained great rewards during the Wars of the Roses and became Lord Chancellor and Archbishop of Canterbury during the reign of King Henry VII (1485–1509). Cardinal Morton arranged the marriage between King Henry VII and Princess Elizabeth of York causing the cessation of the War of the Roses.

He was also notorious for his method of extracting taxes, called 'Morton's Fork', a phrase that would survive until the early-twentieth century. The fork in question had two prongs. One caught those who were rich, and could therefore afford it, and the other skewered those without obvious means, on the basis that they were concealing their money.

In the decoration of the roof the arms of the Morton family are quartered with those of the See of Canterbury. In his will he left money for a priest to say Mass in Bere church for his soul and those of his family.

1505: John Turberville's Bishop Son

John Turberville became lord of the manor of Bere Regis, being the eldest son and heir of John Turberville. He married Isabella, daughter of John Cheverell, and they had five sons; George, James, Roger, Humphrey and Henry, and three daughters; Elizabeth, Edith and Mary. He died in 1536 and was buried in his father's tomb in the church on the orders of his will. Also in the will he bequeathed a farm at Winterborne Whitechurch to his fifth son, Henry, starting that branch of the family.

His second son, James, went to Oxford after Winchester and became a monk. In 1555 he was elected to Bishop of Exeter, being consecrated on 5 September. Bishop James Turberville presided over the See of Exeter in Queen Mary's reign, and who, though a zealous adherent of the Roman Catholic faith, steadfastly refused to abuse his authority in those days of fiery persecution to bring any in his diocese to the stake. Holinshed described Bishop Turberville as:

Very gentle and courteous; most zealous in the Romanish religion, but nothing cruel or bloody. In an age of troubles he was a peacemaker; in an age of persecution he was mild and lenient; amidst overbearing prelates he was an example of meekness; and he showed mercy in prosperity so he found it in adversity.

'This Bishop Turberville carried something of trouble in his name, though nothing but mildness and meekness in his nature,' wrote Thomas Fuller of Broadwindsor in *The History of the Worthies of England*. From Exeter Cathedral he resisted Queen Elizabeth's package of anti-papal measures, refused to take the Oath of Supremacy, and wrote a letter of remonstrance. As a result, on 18 June 1560, he was committed to the Tower of London and though eventually liberated by the Privy Council, on 30 January 1565, he had to find sureties for future 'good behaviour' and his days as a political prelate were effectively over.

James Turberville died in retirement, probably at Bere, in 1570. Sir John Turberville's will, dated 1535, directed that his body should be buried in Bere Church, 'Yn my oun yle before the ymage of our bessid Ladie yn one of the tombs in which Sir Richard Turberville and Sir Robert Turberville, mine ancestors, hath bene buried.' He also directed that the east window of the said aisle should be 'newly made and glazed' as his wife and his executors might decide.

1530: County Divisions

Parishes became Divisions of Counties in 1530 so that civil matters became more unified. Previously there were five ecclesiastical divisions in Dorset. These were Dorchester, Bridport or Beaminster, Blandford North and South, Shafston East and West, and Sherborne (including Sturminster and Cerne). Bere Regis was in the Blandford South division.

1534: Act of Supremacy and a New Vicar

William Wingfield was instituted as vicar of Bere Regis. He resigned in 1545. In 1534 Henry VIII became head of the English Church, breaking with the Roman Church through the Act of Supremacy.

1536: George Turberville

George Turberville became lord of the manor of Bere in 1536, being the eldest son of John Turberville (1505). He married Audrey, daughter of Robert Matthew, Lord Mayor of London and had four sons and six daughters; Robert, Nicholas, Thomas, William, Elizabeth, Edith, Mary, Jane, Dorothy and Lucy. He died in 1547 leaving property to his third son Thomas, at Wool, including Woolbridge manorhouse, which started that branch of the family.

Chapter 3

Reformation and Tudor Bere

1539: Reformation

From the time of the Reformation on 23 March 1539, all church altars were to be taken down. That in Bere church was instead buried under the floor. It was extracted and restored during the church renovation in 1875 by Mr Hibbs, churchwarden. When it was found it reputedly contained some other 'treasures' which were not specified in the churchwardens' accounts. Only four pre-Reformation stone altar-slabs existed in Dorset and being used for their original purpose. These were at Arne, Bere Regis, Corton and Stock Gaylard.

1542: Henry VIII's Muster Roll

The Muster Roll was taken at Bere Regis in 1542 during the reign of Henry VIII. The roll was of able-bodied men, and their weapons, who could be called on in the event of a national emergency. The list was compiled by eminent gentlemen of the neighbourhood. Most of the men were either billmen or archers, the latter of which had to practice once a week to gain or maintain proficiency. These practice sessions were held at the 'butts' on the slopes of Barrow Hill, on the Butt Lane side. Arrows that missed the targets went harmlessly into the earth banks for retrieval.

1545: New Vicar of Bere

William Vallance was instituted as vicar of Bere Regis on 14 July 1545. He was still vicar in 1552 when he signed the inventory of church goods, and probably resigned in 1559. From 1545 until 1558 the patron of the vicarage was Sir Thomas Heneage.

1547: Robert Turberville Unites the Manor

Robert Turberville, eldest son and heir of George Turberville (1536) succeeded his father as lord of the manor. Up until this time the manor had been split between the Turbervilles and the successive Abbesses of Tarrant Abbey until its dissolution in 1539. In 1547 Robert Turberville purchased the other half for £608.16s.8d. and from that moment the Turbervilles held the entire manor.

Robert married Mary, daughter of Roger Maudely of Nunny, Somerset and they had one son Thomas and one daughter Maudlin. He died in 1559 and was buried in the church. A floor tomb slab still exists in the south aisle, but the brass plate originally fixed to it has now been removed to a safer position on the wall nearby. Translated from the Latin it says:

Here lies Robert Turberville, arm bearer, who in his time united the part of the manor of Bere Regis belonging to Tarrant Abbey before its dissolution, to the part which he had inherited from his forefathers who had been lords of this manor from ancient times. Which said Robert died 5 April 1559. Be merciful Christ Jesus. Amen.

1547: Bench-end Carvings

This date is carved on a bench-end of pews in the church. Another bench-end was copied during the restoration of 1875. It bears the inscription '1547, John Day, warden of thys charys.'

There are only five Dorset churches with pre-Reformation stall work, the others being Bradford Abbas, Milton Abbas, Sherborne and Whitchurch Canonicorum, all of which are fragmentary.

1552: Inventory of Church Property

On 16 January a final Commission was set up to consolidate and enforce the sequestering orders since 1539, which was intended to close all the monasteries and confiscate all ornaments, jewellery and goods belonging to churches. Mary I succeeded King Edward VI in 1553 and she cancelled these confiscations. The inventory for Bere Regis was:

Too chalices, havinge but one cover, j shute of vestmentes of redd sylke, j vestment blacke sylke, j vestment with cope of redd sylke, j cope with a albe & decon & subdecon of bustyon, j cope of sudry cullers, j cope redd velvet, j cope of whyt Damaske, garnyshed with bleue velvet, j cope with a vestment for a decon, j albe with decon & subdecon, ij copes one of grene imbrodred with goulde, the other grene, ij Surplices, j lytell bell, iiij belles in the Tower.

The inventory was guaranteed by the vicar, Sir William Valance and Nicholas Grout, John Sargent, Thomas Townberfyld [sic] and George Hart, all confirmed as being honest men of the parish.

stores and stables. Some were packed with grain and hay. A total of 306 men, women and children were left destitute and homeless. An Order of Sessions stated 'that the town of Bere Regis, lately consumed by fire' should receive £50 from the county stock to start an area-wide public appeal to alleviate their distress, the loss due to the fire being assessed at £7,000. A contemporary account stated, 'There was a fier in Bere Regis in 1634, that distressed the inhabitants so that they sent a petishen to the King.'

1635: New Tenants at Bere

Lawrence Squibb and John Loope begin renting property in Bere Regis from 11 June 1635. Gardens and barns were rented for agricultural purposes in Wareham and Bestwall as well. The Bere Regis rent amounted to 6s.8d. Also in 1635 the pair rented tythes of the Golden Prebend of Charminster for 21 years at £4.3s.2d. per annum. Charminster was linked to Bere Regis parish ecclesiastically through Salisbury Diocese.

1637: Latin Epitaph

This is the date of a mural brass to Andrew Loup of Hyde in the south aisle of the church. A long Latin epitaph uses many words of uncertain interpretation, and strange phrases which successfully conceal much of the meaning.

1640: Civil War Parish Records

Several years' worth of the parish records of births, marriages and deaths are missing from those lodged at Salisbury. The Bere Regis originals were all lost in the fire of 4 June 1788 when the vicarage burned together with most of the centre of Bere Regis. Documentation for the whole period of the Civil War is unavailable. The baptisms have a gap of 1640 to 1665; the marriages, 1640–66; and the burials from 1640–55 are missing.

1642: Increased Church Rate

A rate-and-a-half was applied to the church rate payers of Bere Regis in 1642, the first time that this appears in the churchwarden's accounts. The biggest expense of the year was the glazing of the windows (£3.3s.4d.) followed by a huge bill for wine at Easter (£1.13s.8d.), then the gaol money which totalled £1.6s.0d. as usual. Mr Aplin was paid 16s. for keeping the bells and Mr Curry was paid 10s.5d. for four bell ropes. An hour glass was bought for one shilling which may have been a hint to the vicar, and 3s.6d. was paid to put ten crests in the porch, the motifs of which are not recorded. A total of 15s.3d. was dispensed to various distressed people passing through Bere Regis. These were usually people travelling to particular places, sometimes with passes proving their intent, soldiers finding their way home and a significant number of women with children passing through.

The Civil War Years

1642: The Civil War Begins

Arguments over the supremacy of Parliamentary or Royalist factions boiled over into hot war in 1642 with King Charles raising his standard at Nottingham, then the Battle of Edgehill following on 23 October 1642. The result of that was somewhat inconclusive but minor actions followed all over the country including in Dorset. The Parliamentarians, under Cromwell, won a decisive Battle at Marston Moor on 2 July 1644. It was not until 14 June 1645 that the military phase ended at the Battle of Naseby where Cromwell defeated the main Royalist army. King Charles I was executed on 30 January 1649 and Cromwell proclaimed himself Lord Protector of the Commonwealth of England, Scotland and Ireland on 15 December 1653. The Commonwealth ended on 8 May 1660 and King Charles II was restored to the throne.

1644: Manor-House Burned Down

In 1644 the manor-house at Woolbridge was used as a garrison for the Royalist cause during the Civil War, while the house at Bere was set on fire on 18 January 1644 by the Parliamentary forces and in retaliation the King's forces set fire to the house of Sir Walter Erle, a staunch Parliamentarian. In November 1648 John Turberville was accused of:

> ... having supported the king's cause by taking up arms himself, and providing four men and horses under Hopton besides; to have caused Lulworth Castle to be made a royal garrison; to have led a foot company and to have quartered there; to have raised a horse troop for Charles in 1645, to have been in arms at Sherborne when Lord Bedford lay before it, and to have occasioned some to take the King's part, and to have served with Sir Francis Fulford in Wareham garrison.

He was said to be worth £600 a year, and £200 a year un-sequestered. In June 1651, on being pressed for further payment, he claimed that he had already paid £300 in 1643 and £400 since in cattle, corn and other goods. The County Commissioners questioned him further, particularly on his actions in the first war, but he was officially discharged on 20 May 1652 and lived quietly afterwards. After 1660 when Charles II was on the throne, an order of Knights of the Royal Oak was proposed as a reward for those who remained loyal to the King, but the order was not instituted. A total of 617 men nationally were to have been given this honour, with 13 being in Dorset. The values per year of these men's estates was variously quoted as being between £600 to £5,000. Sir John Turberville's estate was valued at £1,500 in that list, somewhat larger than he had claimed in 1648.

1645: Turberville Casualty of War

Sir Troilus Turberville, Captain of Charles I's Cavalry Life Guard, was killed during a skirmish with Parliamentarian forces on the march from Newark to Oxford in October 1645.

Lead pistol shot found at Rye Hill in 2003, probably dating from the seventeenth century.

1646: Kingston Curate Admonished

In the minutes of the Dorset Standing Committee, there is a note to the effect that Mr Kinge, curate of Winterborne Kingston is to cease receiving any more tythes within the parish, it being a part of the parish of Bere Regis. The tythes were the entitlement of Mr Bartholomew Husey, an 'orthodox and devine' vicar of Bere Regis who was to 'quietlie enjoy the same, it being his owne proper due'. It is thought this is dated 9 May, 1646.

1646: New Bere Regis Vicar

Bartholomew Hussey (MA, St Edmund Hall, Oxford) becomes vicar of Bere Regis on being nominated by the House of Lords on 19 August. He died on 7 March 1649. The benefice was vacant until 1654, but the village was served by Thomas King, while he was still the curate of Winterborne Kingston. From 1646 until 1662 the patron of the vicarage was Thomas Strangways. Minutes dated 16 March 1648 of the Dorset Standing Committee, noted that the vicar Mr Bartholomew Hussey, lately deceased, owed over £100 to George Mullens and William Bolter. There was an order for the two to receive £30 out of the rents, tythes and profits of the vicarage until 24 June next. The remainder of the tythe money was to be used to pay rates and taxes on the vicarage, and to provide 'a minister to teach the people, and pay him after the rate of tenne shillings every weeke for his labor and paines in that behalfe'.

1646: Philliols Farm Sequestered

Puritan ascendancy in November 1646, after the upheavals of Civil War, resulted in Philliols Farm being sequestered from a 'delinquent' Jeffrey Samways. The county treasurer was authorised to pay £32 'out of the rents and profits' to Captain James Dewy, towards reimbursement for a debenture 'laid out in the service of the State'. Revd Benjamin Hussey, as 'an able an orthodox divine', was appointed vicar of Bere Regis 'of which [Winterborne] Kingston is a member'. On the ground, however, there were others who staked their claims. John Franklin the elder, Stephen Plucknett, William Bolter senr and William Bolter junr were in dispute in April 1647 concerning 'the barn and tithes' in Bere Regis. Franklin held the rights and maintained that Plucknett had defaulted on a lease, with rent arrears, resulting in its termination. It was adjudicated by Dorset Standing Committee that Plucknett held a valid lease which he could continue to enjoy, provided he paid rent 'unto the said Franklin, any other or former order notwithstanding'.

1648: Manor-House Repaired

This is the date carved on a stone which Hutchins found below a window at the back of the manor-house when he visited in the eighteenth century. After the house was demolished, the stone, as rubble, was eventually used to strengthen the banks of the river nearby, and until the 1970s it was built into a small low wall near the west entrance to the water-cress beds. After the 1970s the stone was removed during renovations of the river walling.

1648: Outlaw George Moreton

On 14 December, Philippa Banckworth, widow of John Banckworth, leased the manors of Shitterton, Milborne St Andrew, Winterborne Kingston, Whatcombe, and also Clenstone Farm, all formerly of George Moreton, Bart., for one year at 40s.8d. on the declaration of Moreton's outlawed actions on the Royalist side during the war.

1652: Kingston Autonomy Proposal

The Augmentation Books making a Tabular Statement of Union and Division of Parishes noted that the parish of Beare [sic] Regis was to be separated from Kingston and that Kingston chapel was to become a parish church. Also stated was that Turners Puddle was joined to Beare [sic] Regis, while the inhabitants of Anderson were to join with Kingston.

1653: Church Affairs Back to Normal

The churchwardens' accounts for 1653 show that there was £6.6s.11d left over from the previous year, which with other items including a gift from John Speare via Thomas Lucas of £2 brought the total income to £10.18s.11d. The largest payment of the year was £2.18s.6d. for the gaol money, while the glazier was paid £2.2s for window repairs. A repair job on the clapper in the little bell together with repairs or new bell ropes came to an additional 16s.9d. John Read was paid £1 for ringing the bell and keeping the clock and a further 2s.6d. for oil and straps for the bells. The ringers were paid 8s.6d for 5 November. Along with many small payments Mr Dunt was paid 2s. for 'laying' two graves and 2d. was paid to William Welch for mending the beare. The total spending of £9.17s.5d. was audited as correct on 10 May 1654.

1654: Moreton's Further Setbacks
From 13 February, Owen Owens, gent., of Carmarthan, leased the manors of Milborne St Andrew, Shitterton, Winterborne Kingston, Whatcombe and Clenston Farm, all formerly properties of Sir George Morton of Clenstone, during the term of his outlawry at 21s.9½d. per annum.

1654: New Vicar
Philip Lamb (BA, Clare College, Cambridge) became the vicar of Bere Regis on 3 April 1654, but was ejected from his position, for Congregationalist practices, in 1662. He went to Alton Pancras in central Dorset, but returned to East Morden in 1672. From there, Lamb crossed the hills to resume regular preaching at Winterborne Kingston, drawing large congregations, until being ousted again and moving to London. He established his own church at Clapham.

1654: Stranger Burial at Bere
The church rate raised a total of £9.16s.1d. plus a burial fee from Colett Trew of 6s.8d. for her daughter. A travelling seaman passing through the village was sick so was put up at publican Thomas Joyner's house and died on 6 May. Burial costs, including a shroud, cost the parish 6s.6d. Numerous travellers were helped during the year, as usual being paid 6d. to help them on their way. The normal payments for the year were the gaol money (£2.12s.), the ringers for 5 November (8s.4d.), John Read for keeping the clock and ringing the curfew bell (£1.2s.) and keeping the bells (13s.). The bells received more attention, such as leather for the clappers (15s.4d.), John Curry for more bell ropes (4s.6d.), John Daw for a new clapper for the little bell (11s.10d.) and a bell rope for the fourth bell (3s.). Ten shillings was paid for a bible clasp and silk strings, which brought total spending to £10.4s.11d.

1656: Triple Church Rate
The churchwardens raised a triple church rate in 1656 totalling £38.10s.11d., which included about £7 from burials, gifts and arrears. Extensive work in the belfry was carried out which included the re-casting of bells and the construction of a new bell cage. The little bell was cast from 721lb (327kg) of metal, then 145lb (66kg) of new metal was added to the second bell followed by 29lb (13kg) more a little later, which together with other bell modifications cost £16.1s.0d. Clock repairs included more iron bracing and wires with pulleys. Also the 'iron plummet' was remade. The total spend in 1656 came to £46.9s.0d., figures of which were audited on 6 May 1658.

The second bell in the church tower has the following inscription:

AL*THOUGHT*THAT*I *AM-BVT-SMALL*
YET-I*BE*HARD-A-BOVE*THEM-ALL*
AL*ID*C*W ANNODOMINI*1656-TP

1659: Murder in London
Major George Strangways, the second son of John Strangways, had been left the farm at Mussen when his father died, in about 1649. However, he went to live in Blandford. His 'ancient' sister, Mabel Strangways, borrowed money from George to stock the farm. George expressed disgust when Mabel married widower John Fussel and threatened 'to be the death of him' and then put this into effect when he found they were 'endeavouring to defraud him of part of his estate, besides the money due by bond'. There had been a verbal confrontation followed by the offer of a dual which, wisely, Fussel declined.

The killing took place at John Fussel's London lodging, at the George and Half-Moon, as he sat 'at his desk, with his face towards the window' at ten o'clock at night, with the curtain almost completely drawn, save for a slight gap. Through this the marksman took steady aim and fired three bullets from a carbine. One struck Fussel through the forehead, 'and the other in about his mouth; the third bullet or slug stuck in the lower part of the timber of the window'.

George Strangways was arrested and committed for trial before Lord Chief Justice Glynn, but refused to plead, in the default of which was sentenced to 'the terror of the death his obstinate silence would enforce them to inflict upon him'. On returning to Newgate, to the Press Yard, he wrote to another brother-in-law, Major Dewie MP, from the shadow of his 'pressing death' to say he was provoked by Fussel's 'insufferable wrongs' and intended 'by the discharging of a warning piece to have only terrified his heart from practising litigious suites' and offered his own death 'one to my maker, the other to the law'.

In the dungeon, in January 1659, he took leave of his friends, kneeled in prayer, and was then laid out with weights:

... which finding too light for a sudden execution, many of those standing by, added their burthens to disburthen him of his pain, which notwithstanding for the time of its continuance, as it was to him a dreadful sufferance, so was it to them a horrid spectacle, his dying groans filling the uncoath dungeon with the voice of terror. That the prisoner be sent to the place from whence he came; and that he be put into a mean house stopped from any light; and that he be laid upon his back, with his body bare, saving something to cover his privy parts: That his arms shall be stretched forth with a cord, the one to one side of the prison, the other to the other side of the prison; and in the like manner shall his legs be used: And that upon his body shall be

laid as much iron and stone as he can bear, and more; and the first day shall he have three morsels of barley bread, and the next day shall he drink thrice of the water in the next channel to the prison door, but no spring or fountain water: And this shall be his punishment till he die.

In eight to ten minutes he was dead, and his body put on public display in a coffin:

... that many standers by beheld the bruise made by the press, whose triangular form, being placed with the acute angle about the region of the heart, did soon deprive that fountain of life of its necessary motion, though he was prohibited that usual favour in that kind, to have a sharp piece of timber layed under his back, to accelerate its penetration.

The place-name Mussen in a pamphlet published in 1659 has been identified as Winterbourne Musten, formerly in the parish of Bere Regis but now a hamlet between Winterborne Kingston and Anderson. The *Unhappy Marksman*, the publication in question, has a lengthy sub-title:

A perfect and impartial discovery of that late barbarous and unparalleled murder committed by Mr George Strangways, formerly a Major in the King's Army, on his brother-in-law Mr John Fussel, an attorney, on Friday the 11th of February [1658]. *Together with a full discovery of the fatal cause of those unhappy differences which first occasioned the suits in law betwixt them. Also the behaviour of Mr Strangways at his trial. The dreadful sentence pronounced against him. His letter to his brother-in-law, a member of Parliament. The words by him delivered at his death; and his stout, but Christian-like method of dying.*

After The Restoration of the Monarchy

1662: Hearth Taxes
The hearth tax was another method to raise money, and was based on the number of fireplaces in a person's house. The Hundred of Beere [sic] had 223 hearths suitable for taxation at one shilling each, and the rate was payable twice a year, at Ladyday (25 March) and Michealmas (29 September). Therefore £22.6s. was raised each year. However, by the end of 1664 it was proving too uneconomic to collect and constantly monitor and there were no collections in 1665. It is of interest to note that at Court Green, John Turberville had 16 hearths, four of which he had sealed up or 'stopt' as it is recorded in the 1662 assessment.

1663: Replacement Vicar
Thomas Basket (BA) was instituted as vicar of Bere Regis on 23 January after the ejection of Philip Lamb. He died in 1665. During Thomas Basket's incumbency a new chalice was made. It is made of silver

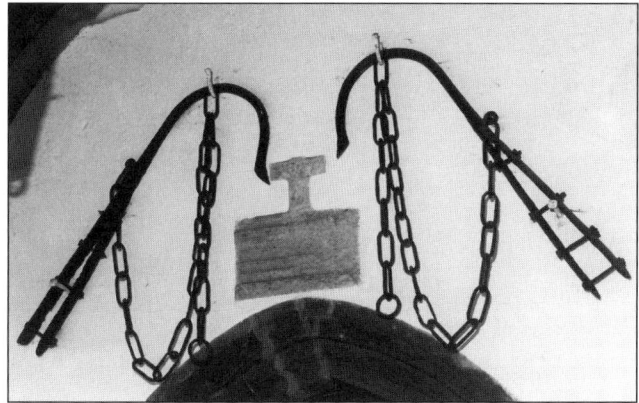

Iron 'fire-hooks' in the church porch. Dating from the seventeenth century they were for pulling thatch to create a fire break. The wooden handles have long-since gone.

and is 6.75ins high and almost 4ins across at the lip. It is used to offer wine at Holy Communion.

1665: Another New Vicar
Robert Frampton became the vicar of Bere Regis on 4 December, but resigned less than a year later. In both 1662 and 1665 the patron of the vicarage was Giles Strangways.

1665: More Black Death
The Black Death again resulted in many deaths. This time, cats and dogs were killed in the hope that this would reduce the transmission of the disease. The rats, the real carriers, were not exterminated, and without their natural predators, the disease spread more easily.

1666: Another Vicar
Lewis White was instituted vicar of Bere Regis on 23 October 1666, and was buried on 8 November 1667. From 1666 until 1699 the patron of the vicarage was Henry Whitaker.

1668: Yet Another Vicar
John Cupper was instituted vicar of Bere Regis on 14 April 1668. He recruited a curate, Thomas Aylesbury, who was instituted on 3 August 1672, and either died or resigned in 1674.

1668: Token Money at Bere
William Lodge, a trader of Beare [sic], issued his own coinage, particularly half pennies. This was despite a law passed on 12 May 1594 prohibiting the minting of coins without authority in England. Token coins fulfilled a need as the official coin supply disappeared.

1672: Thomas Turberville
Thomas Turberville (1621–1701) became lord of the manor of Bere Regis, being the brother of Sir John Turberville (1633). He married Elizabeth (buried 30 August 1686), daughter of Thomas Baskett of Dewlish, and there were three children, Thomas, Robert and Elizabeth (buried 8 October 1681). He was

Warren House, numbered 136 and 137 in the manorial system, was two dwellings in the seventeenth century and enlarged in the nineteenth. The building appears on the 1777 map of Drax property, but the first mention of the Warren name in the parish register is Charles Warren whose son William was buried on 27 December 1667. The name could equally have derived from rabbiting and have no connected to the Warren family.

patron of the incumbency of Milborne St Andrew in 1680, and Sheriff of Dorset in 1686. In 1692 he was a churchwarden of Bere Regis, and it appears from the accounts of that year that he overspent by about £19 during his term of office, when a large amount of repair work was carried out on the church. He was buried on 30 May 1701.

1674: White Lovington
White Lovington was first mentioned in the parish records: 'On 2 March 1674, Mary daughter of Richard Woolfreys of White Lovington, was baptised.'

1674: Edmund Strangways Becomes Vicar
Edmund Strangways (BA, Hart Hall, Oxford) was instituted vicar of Bere Regis on 10 May 1675. He had signed the register transcript in 1674 shortly after he was instituted. He was buried on 13 July 1678.

1679: Vicar Begins 19-Year Service
Mr John Ouctherlony (MA, St Andrews) was instituted as vicar of Bere Regis on 1 January and served for 19 years. He had six children: Lenseo (baptised 6 January

1680), John (14 February 1682), Thomas (15 May 1684), William (2 July 1685), Mary (baptised 20 October 1687; burial 30 April 1688), and a second Mary (baptised 8 September 1693). The vicar resigned in 1698.

1683: Travellers Assisted
The spending of the churchwardens for 1683 totalled £11.19s.3d. and included most of the usual expenses. There were payments made to three travellers in particular; the first being to two people who were 'cast away coming from Virginia'. Another payment was made to three travellers 'who came from Tangier and had his majesties passes', while the third was to two men who were formerly slaves. Clock and bell repairs featured through the year while the ringers were paid and given beer for 'ye day of thanksgiving for his majesties and his royal brother's deliverance.' The ringers received 14s.

1684: New Bell for the Church
The churchwardens' accounts for 1684 show yet more bell repairs but the bell founder was paid £16.10s.0d. for casting another bell. Later more metal was added

36

to get the tuning correct. Repairs to the tower and the belfry was another significant expense, while John Gould was paid 15s. to provide half a hogshead of beer for the ringers at 'ye proclamation of ye king'.

1684: Thomas Turberville Withholds Rate

Details of Thomas Turberville's non-payment of the church rate are noted in a statement made by the churchwardens, dated 16 May 1684:

These are to certify all whom it may or shall any wayes hereafter concerne That Thomas Turbervile of Beer Regis in the County of Dorstt and peculiar Jurisdiccon of the Revd Deane of Sarum, Esqr, was prsented at the last Visitation by the Churchwardens of the sd parish for not paying his Rates towards the repacon of the said Church of Beere Regis aforesaid, Whereupon the said Mr Turbervile was cited to the Deane of Sarum's Court, he, appearing by his proctor, denyed the said presentmt to be true, then Notice was given thereof to the Churchwardens, but they never prosecuted the busines any farther, whereupon the said Mr Turbervile was dismissed from the said presentment. In testimony of the trueth hereof Wee have hereunto sett our hands this sixteenth day of May 1684.

It is signed by George Frome and Hugo Frome.

1685: Church Porch Improved

The churchwardens oversaw the spending of £55.5s.2½d during 1685. Major work was carried out on new pews but the majority was spent on repairs to the porch including new lead for the roof and a lot of timber replacement. The ringers were paid and given beer on three occasions in particular. These were 'when the Duke was routed', 'on ye King's birthday', and St George's day. A new cover for the font had cost 5s., while a cork for the font had cost 6d. on 5 July 1685.

1686: Sir John Morton Sued

The surplices were washed at 'Woodburytide' according to the churchwardens' accounts for 1686. Oil and candles for the King's birthday on 14 October cost 2s.10d., then 3s.7d. was paid for beer and candles for the ringers on 6 February that being Coronation Day (for James II). It was noted that Thomas Turberville owed 18s.11d. at the end of the year, while Mr ffrome [sic] was paid 3s.4d. for appearing in court against Sir John Morton for non-payment of the church rate.

The buildings at Buddens Farm once consisted of three sides of a quadrangle and dated from about the 1780s. The first mention of the name Budden appears in the parish registers on 20 January 1686 when John Budden the elder was buried.

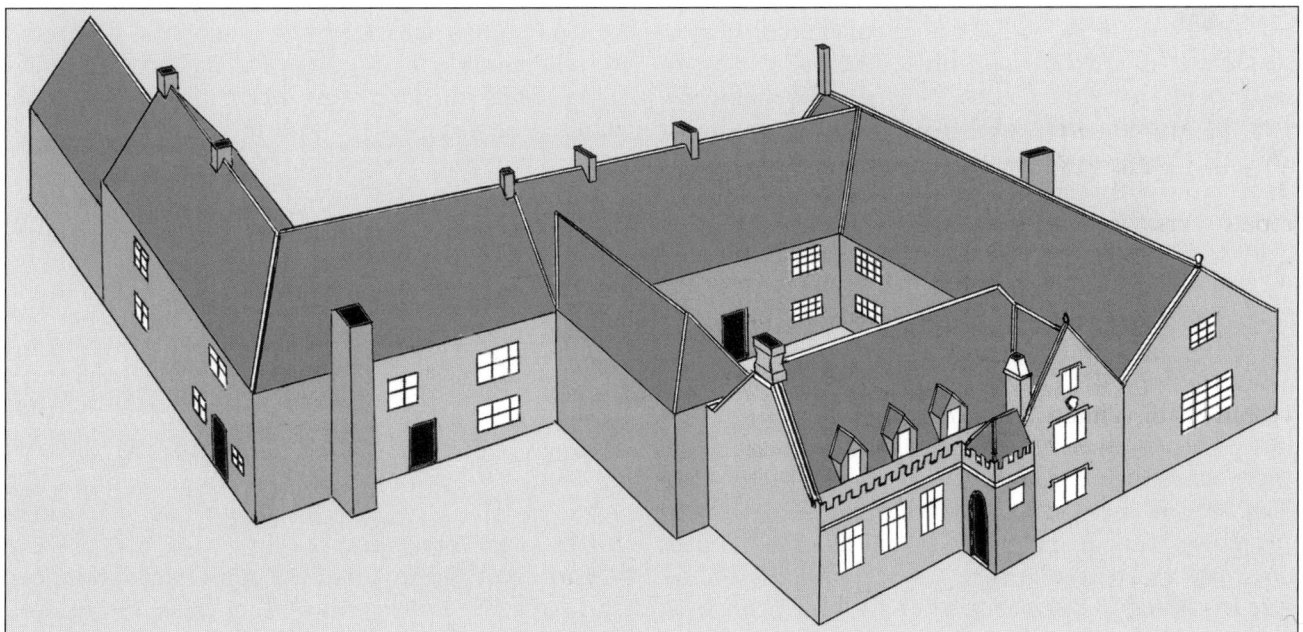

Impression of how the Court Green manor-house would have looked between 1650 and the 1780s. The Great Hall with embattled parapets is based on the engraving used in Hutchins's book, while the quadrangle is based on an ink-and-wash painting from the east dated 1786. The position of all the buildings was established by a resistivity survey conducted in January 2004.

1687: Tollervill Family Recorded

A proclamation and order for thanksgiving for the Queen's conception was bought by the churchwardens and this was followed by a thanksgiving day ringing session for which the ringers received 2s.6d. Window glazing in the church came to £1.12s.6d, while John Tollervill sold them a bell rope for 4s.2d.

1688: 225 Military Travellers

According to the churchwardens' accounts for 1688, a total of 79 soldiers and 146 seamen came through Bere Regis and were assisted on their way. There was a serious storm during the year which the wardens called 'the great wind'. Repairs to the church indicate how strong this wind was. It lifted lead sheets on the roof which had to be put back, several windows were blown in and had to have glass refitted, and repairs were made after the 'church foundered'. The north and south windows seem to have borne the brunt of the storm. The 'great gate' was also mended, costing 2s.6d.

1688: Thomas Williams Moves to Bere Regis

Thomas Williams moved to Bere Regis at Shitterton House, from Morlaix in Brittany where he was in business. Williams was known for making many notes in pocket books between 1688 and 1701, and later founded a charity to help with funds to further the education of the young and poor of Bere Regis. He died in 1728 and is buried in Bere Regis church.

1690: New Bible is Major Purchase

The ringers were paid on 10 November for Thanksgiving Day and they also received payment for ringing on 'gunpowder treason day' according to the churchwardens' accounts. Major expenses during the year were for repairing both the roof leads and the church windows. Mr William Churchill was paid £2.15s. for a new bible.

1692: Land Tax for Bere

The assessments for land tax in and around the village were as follows: Beer Regis (£196.6s.8d.), Hyde (£23.6s.0d.), Kingshold (£21.16s.0d.) and Shitterton (£34.15s.9d.).

1692: Major Church Roof Repairs

The churchwardens' accounts show that in 1692 there were major repairs carried out on the church roof which included £13.6s.7d. for lead and the plumber. Timber had cost £8.13s., which included 500ft of oak boards. It is not clear where the building work was done on the church but 200 bushels (1,600 gallons) of lime and 7,000 bricks were purchased for a total of £8.10s.10d. The daily pay for semi-skilled men seems to have been about 1s.3d.

The ringers were paid 6s. to ring when the French Fleet was beaten.

1693: New Silver Paten

Amongst the usual expenditure by the churchwardens for 1693 there was 4s. paid to the ringers when the Fleet was beaten in action off Cape St Vincent (16 June), and a shilling was given to 'a poore man that his tongue was cut out of his head.' The church plate includes a silver paten with hallmarks of the date 1693. Its diameter is 9.125ins and it is 2.375ins high. It was used to offer bread at Holy Communion.

1695: Popish Plot Discovered

Richard Williams and Richard Stagg were paid a shilling for tolling the bell as Queen Mary was buried, according to the churchwardens' accounts. Nicholas Hutching was paid £1.12s. 'for soldering of ye leads' on the church roof. Another 2s. was paid for a book and proclamation for a thanksgiving for 'ye Discovery of ye popish plot'.

1696: Moreton Withholds Payment

The usual mending and repairing of the church features heavily in the churchwardens' accounts for 1696. There were a lot of travellers coming through Bere Regis this year, including many ex-prisoners from France making their way back home. They were usually given 6d. to move them on. Ten church rate payers had not paid their tax including Sir John Morton who still owed 2s.6d. for Chamberlaynes Heath at the end of the year.

1698: New Tenor Bell

The biggest expense of 1698, from the churchwardens' accounts, was £29.0s.7d. for work connected with the tenor bell. The new bell had cost £16, paid to Mr Tosier, for the casting alone. The church plate included a silver paten with the hallmark date of 1698. It is 6.5ins in diameter and 1.5ins high and is used by the priest to offer bread at communion services. The accounts show that it had cost 18s. The tenor bell in the church tower has the following inscription:

IOHN:OVGHTRELONEYVICKER*IVSTENYEN
EKENS:AND:IOHN:HASZARD:CHURCH:
WARDENS-CLEMANT:TOSIEAR*
CAST-MEE*IN*1698*THIS:BELL*WAS THE GIVEFT
OF MARY DYET

1699: Bere's New Vicar

William Abell (MA, Balliol College, Oxford) becomes the vicar of Bere Regis on 13 May 1699. He died on 22 April 1701. From 1699 until 1704 the patron of the vicarage was Roger Mander DD, master of Balliol College, Oxford.

Chapter 5

The Eighteenth Century

1701: Thomas Turberville

Thomas Turberville succeeded to the manor of Bere Regis, being the eldest son of Thomas Turberville (1672). He married, in about 1695, Mary, daughter of Thomas Trenchard and they had four sons and three daughters. All four sons died young, Thomas (buried 11 February 1699), John (buried 7 June 1701), Robert (buried 27 February 1702) and George (buried 7 May 1703). Their three daughters, Mary and twins Frances and Elizabeth survived him after his death on 3 February 1705 and burial on 18 February 1705.

1701: New Vicar Instituted

William Hockin (MA, Balliol College, Oxford) became vicar of Bere Regis. He was instituted on 7 July 1701 and was buried on 7 February 1710.

1701: Refugees from France

Sick seamen were still passing through Bere Regis from France during 1701 according to the churchwardens' accounts. Major re-glazing work on the church windows was carried out with Edward Moores being paid a total of £3.15s.2d. for his labour and materials. The plumber was paid £5.3s.9d. for lead repairs on the roof and probably for the window soldering. The sum of 4s. was paid to John Tollerville for a bell rope, while 2s. was spent on tiles for a porch repair job.

Tunnels discovered under Court Green Farm in August 1981.

1703: Severe Storm Hits Bere

There was another severe storm which hit Bere Regis in 1703. The churchwardens' accounts reveal that 'the Wind blew up' and roof leads had to be layed down again. The windows were damaged too and Matthew Moores was paid £2.13s.8d. for glazing work. John Tollerville made another 4s.6d. by selling the wardens more bell rope. The plumber's wages had been 2s.6d. per day.

1704: Mary, Frances and Elizabeth Turberville

For the first time heiresses succeeded as owners of the manor of Bere Regis. Mary, Frances and Elizabeth Turberville were the daughters of Thomas Turberville (1701); all four of his sons had died as children. Mary married Major William Ducket in 1721, and died a widow, buried on 3 September 1739 aged about 40.

From 1704 the churchwardens' accounts show that the rates of parochial duties normally entered as being from the lord of the manor were noted as being from 'The Widow & Coheirs of Esqr Turberville'. The three sisters sold the manor to Henry Drax in 1733, but didn't move out until their mother died in 1739. Frances and Elizabeth moved to London and continued to be inseparable, neither marrying. They lived at Pursers Cross, Fulham and died within days of each other, aged 77 and were buried together at Putney on the same day in February 1780.

1709: New Seats and a Fifth Bell

The churchwardens' accounts of 1709 record a lot of church expenses on the seats and the bells. Some 60 deal boards were bought from Mrs Seaward for £4.10s then Edward Meader and John Ash were paid £5.10s.6d to build the new seats in the church. The second and fourth bells were re-cast and the transportation costs alone came to £4.15s. Thomas Knight was paid £17 for re-casting the bells and 162lb (73.5kg) of new metal costing £9.7s. was added to the bill. The fifth bell in the church tower has the following inscription:

ROBERT FRAMPTON*THOMAS*FRAMPTON*
ANNO:DOMINI*1709 – THOMAS*KNIGHT*
WILLIAM* KNIGHT*****

There seems to have been a dispute regarding the money for the bell foundry as Mr ffrome [sic] was paid 1s.6d. for dismissing the Prosecution regarding some aspect of the payment. Mr Waters was paid £3.14s.6d. for mending the church roof leads and Dr Moores' bill for glazing in 1708–09 amounted to £2.13s.6d.

1710: The Turberville Vault
The east end of the south aisle of the church at Bere Regis has many tombs of several types which are nearly all for the Turberville family. The stained-glass window on the south of the aisle has the coats of arms of the family and those of the families that married Turbervilles, but this is a later repair, paid for by Mrs Drax in 1875. There is a large stone floor slab 7ft by 3ft 6ins (2.1m x 1.05m) in the south aisle as well. This bears the now-worn inscription *Ostium Sepulchri Antiquae Familiae Turberville, 24 Junii, 1710,* or 'Door of the Sepulchre of the Ancient Family of the Turbervilles' and was sealed after the reburial of the remains of the four sons and one daughter of Thomas Turberville, all in one coffin. The burial vault would remain undisturbed for the next 165 years.

Also in the south aisle there is a bricked-up doorway which would provide access directly into the Turberville pews in the church. Tradition in the village has it that a Turberville lord of the manor had an altercation with the vicar and vowed never to enter through the church doors. After making up with the vicar, and in order not to break his vow, he added another door.

1711: New Vicar and Balliol Patronage
John Wills (MA, Balliol College, Oxford) was instituted vicar of Bere Regis on 19 April 1711. According to the Dean's subscription book he resigned in 1725 to practice medicine. He was buried on 22 March

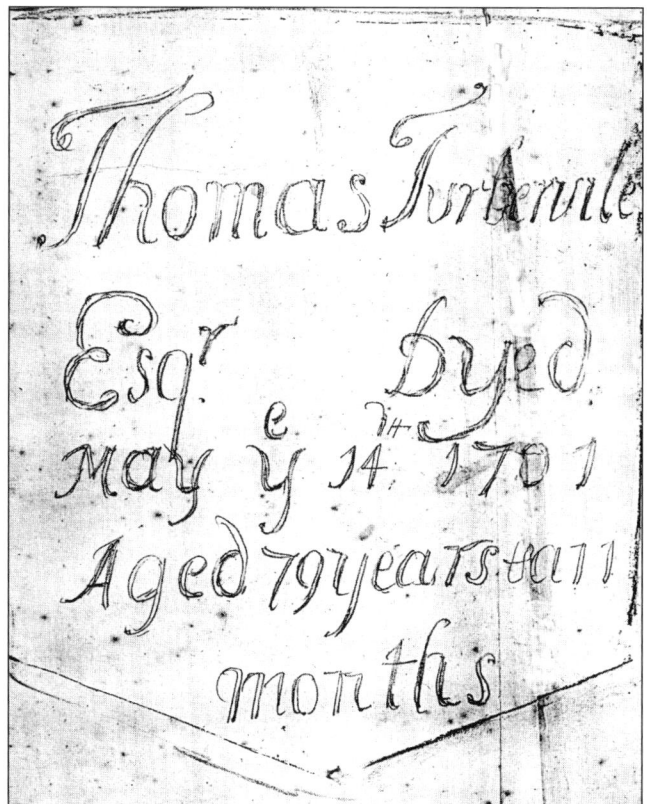

1726. In 1704, and in accordance with the will of Roger Mander, the patronage of the vicarage had passed to the master and fellows of Balliol College, Oxford and has remained unchanged since then. Meanwhile, 'Leckyers' in Bere Regis – location probably Blind Street and obviously the home of the Lockyer family – was licensed for Presbyterian worship in 1711.

1712: The Royal Oak Pub
The Royal Oak is first mentioned as such in 1712, although this alehouse had been in operation since

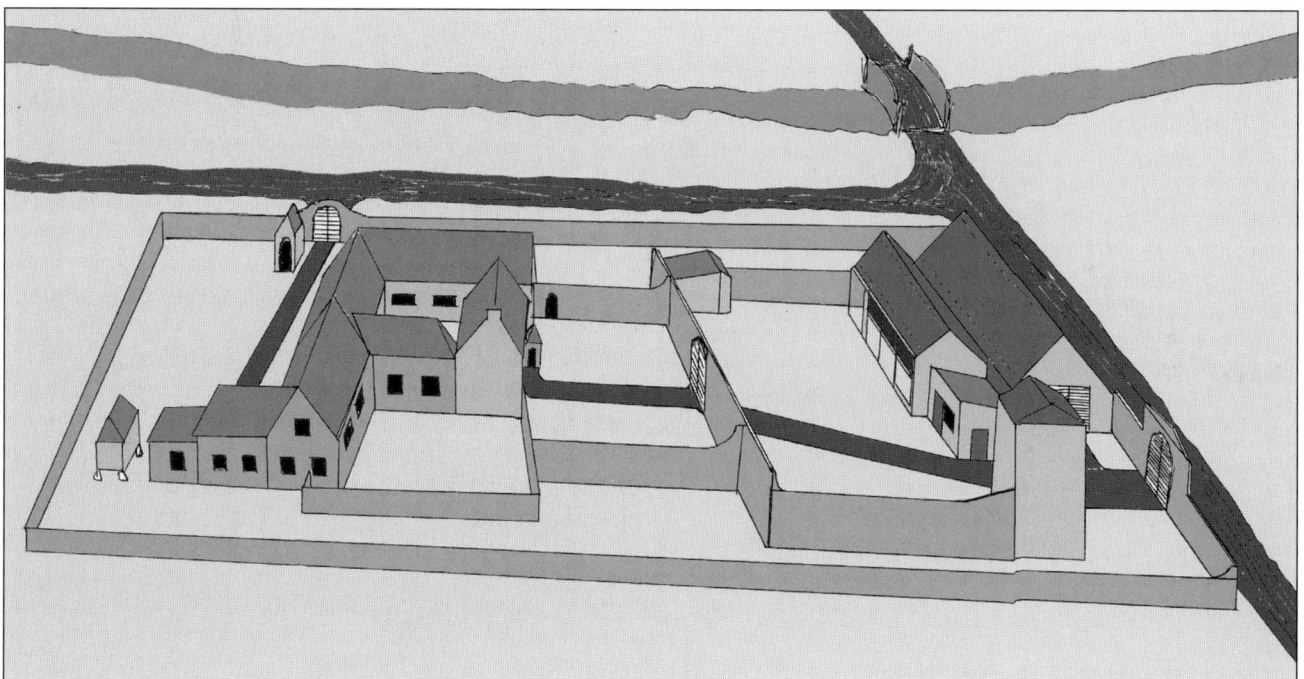

Robert Turberile Esqr Dyed May ye 6th 1710 In ye 37 year of his age

In This Coffine Remaines All that is left of 4 sons & on daughter of Thomas Turberuile Land Esqwhich was entred In this vault June ye 24 1710

Tuberville Tombs. Bere Regis Church

Opposite page, top: *Pencil rubbing of the plaque on the coffin of Thomas Turberville who died on 14 May 1701.*

Opposite page, bottom: *Impression of the complete complex of buildings at Court Green as it would have looked from the north between 1650 and 1750. The manor-house and walled gardens to the left are attached to the building that still exists. The outer enclosure included a smithy, stables and the tithe barn adjacent to the road, now Southbrook. The entrance and gate offered high security, some of which remained until the late-eighteenth century.*

This page, top left: *The plaque on the coffin of Robert Turberville was pencil-rubbed when the vault was opened in about 1875. He had died on 6 May 1710 aged 37.*

This page, top right: *Pencil rubbing of the plaque on the coffin of the four sons and one daughter of Thomas Turberville, interred in the Turberville vault on 24 June 1710.*

Above right: *East end of the south aisle in the church contains Turberville tombs.*

Right: *The Royal Oak pictured in May 1991.*

about 1611. At that time Peter Melmouth ran the business; then from about 1650 the Joyner family ran the pub which was known as 'Joyners' even after the name Royal Oak was formally adopted. The current building is that which was rebuilt after the fire of 1788. The previous structure was similar in size and shape according to the 1777 map. From 1710, until the present day, the Royal Oak has been tenanted rather than being run by the owner of the property.

1713: Ladies of the Manor
The ladies of the manor are mentioned in connection with the church rate for this year. These were the surviving daughters of Thomas Turverville. The churchwardens' accounts for 1713–14 also show that Thomas Biswell was paid £2 for 'a Tree to rope ye Church', the meaning of which is unknown.

1714: A New King
The ringers were paid 6s.6d. at the proclamation of King George I (1 August 1714) and a further 13s.6d. for ringing on coronation day. George Moores charged £1.7s.6d. for glazing the church windows.

1715: The Duke William Pub
There was an alehouse at Shitterton from 1715 until 1759, probably called The Duke William. Locally it is thought that it was situated where No. 12 Shitterton is now located, between the path to Black Hill and Shitterton Farm. Christopher Kerley was the licensee in 1715 and Robert Talbot had it when it closed in 1759.

1716: The King Returns
The churchwardens' accounts show that a lot of maintenance work went on around the church, particularly on the porch, the belfry window and other church windows. Major expenses included brick and timber. The ringers were paid and a bonfire was made for celebrations 'when ye King came home' then later for a 'rejoicing day'. The audit date for the figures is 11 July 1717.

1717: The Greyhound Pub
The Greyhound alehouse was situated in the gap between No. 83 West Street and No. 84 (the current Post Office) from 1717 to 1766. The licensee in 1717 was William Stagg. It closed when Richard Stagg ceased trading in 1766.

1717: Fire in Bere Regis
There was a serious fire in the village that destroyed 14 houses. No other details are known.

1717–18: Roof Lead Repairs
A total of £51.14s.5d. was raised by the churchwardens for this accounting period (Easter to Easter). Major lead work on the church was carried out by Richard Ham of Milton, for which he was paid £20.6s.6d. This included the price of the lead sheet. Five bottles of wine at Easter cost 12s.6d. and the surplice was mended six times for 3s.6d. Matthew Moores was paid £1.10s. for more glazing work around the church. The ringers were paid 2s.6d. for the anniversary of King George's coronation day.

1719: New Church Clock
The clock in Bere Regis church had the following inscription: 'Robert Frampton and Joshua Gollop Church Wardens. Lawrence Boyce Fecit, 1719'. Lawrence Boyce was a blacksmith from Puddletown. The clock is now preserved in Dorset County Museum at Dorchester.

1719: Barrow Hill Boys' School
The first free school for village children, endowed by Thomas Williams, was established on Barrow Hill. Its foundation dates back to Williams's will, in 1719, in which he provided for the clothing and teaching of six boys. The Charity School formally came into the Anglican orbit on being incorporated as a National School under the wing of the snappily-titled National Society for Promotion the Education of the Poor in the Principles of the Established Church.

1719: Thomas Williams Trust
Thomas Williams, Esq., donated, by deed, in trust, 7 acres of land in Beer fields, a dwelling-house, orchard and 6 acres of pasture at Rye Hill, two dwelling-houses, two gardens, one orchard and two grounds of 4 acres, a cottage at Bugbarrow with half an acre of land belonging thereto, some pasture, and also the tithe of hay of a moor on the west side of the little meadow on the south end of Rush Mead. The rents and profits from the above were to be used for the teaching and clothing of six poor boys born in Bere Regis parish. The house at Bugbarrow was rebuilt as a school, while the annual produce raised £8.11s.4d.

Henry Fisher, clerk, donated £100 in his will dated 1773 – vested in John Bond Esq. In 1785 Mrs Nevill Pleydell gave £5 – vested with the vicar, while financial donations were made by the following: George Daw (£10), James Penny (£5), William Penny (£10), John Frome, gent. (£10), Thomas Clench (£5), Mathew Turberville, gent. (£5), John Turberville, Esq.,(£10), George Turberville, gent. (£2.10s.), Clothier Bragge (£5), Eliz. Galton, widow (£10), Robert Williams, Esq. (£10), John Phillips (£5), John Loop (£5), Henry Creech (£5), Nicholas Merefield (£5), making a total of £102. Further donations were made by Richard Mitchell, gent., (£10), William Gould, merchant (£2), Capt. Thomas Squibb (£5), Mr Lawrence Squibb (£1), but somehow £18 of the total went missing, the remainder being put in the charge of the heirs of the late Thomas Erle Drax, Esq.

The interest from the first sum was used to distribute to the poor of the village, while the latter sum's

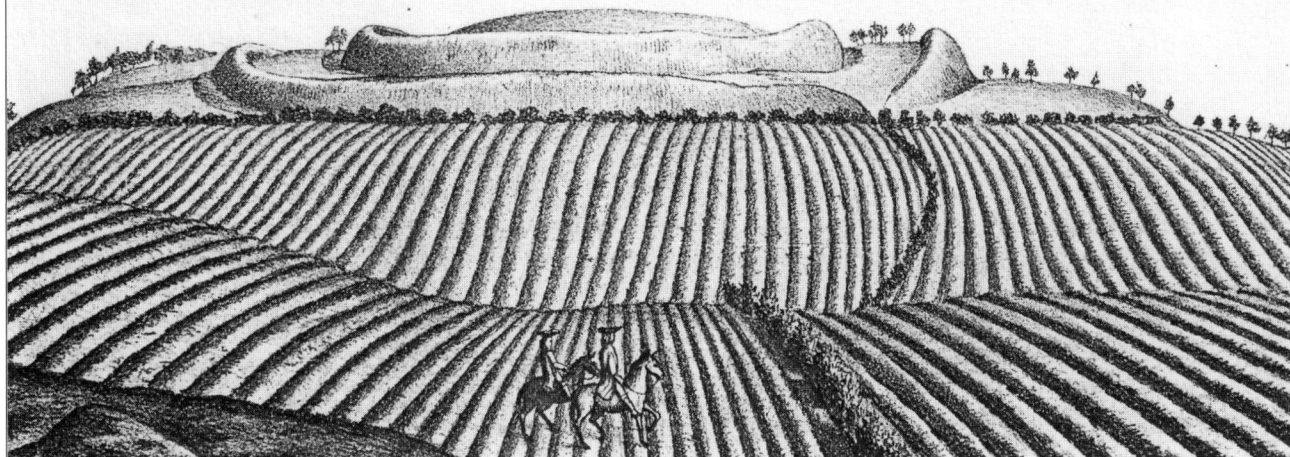

A 1724 engraving of Woodbury Hill from the south, dated 9 June. William Stukeley did the original drawing from which Elisha Kirkall made the engraving, which was used in Stukeley's **Itinerarium Curiosum.**

interest was specifically for poor children. Bernard Mitchell's will, dated 22 March 1646, had pledged rental charges for the benefit of the poor of the parish, via his properties at Melcombe Regis. This was incorporated into the Williams Trust fund.

Mrs Barbara Skinner's will of 1769 gave £200 for the dissenting poor, at the discretion of her executor, Mr George Brugh.

A stone plaque on the old Boys' School, Barrow Hill, reads: 'BERE SCHOOL, ENDOWED BY THOS WILLIAMS Esq. A.D. 1719.' The building contains a wooden beam with the date 1721. The management of the Trust fund was so successful that it still exists today as the Thomas Williams Educational Foundation Trust.

1719–20: New Book of Common Prayer
Over £51 was raised by the churchwardens for this year, but spending totalled over £54. A lot of seamen that were 'cast away' passed through the village and most were given 6d., although if a group passed through together they received less proportionately. A new Common Prayer Book was purchased for £4.6s.8d. – a huge sum at the time, while bread for communion for two years was paid for and came to 4s. Matthew Moores' bill for glazing came to £2.2s.2d. and David Compton was paid 4s.8d. for mending the church seats.

1721: Bere Presbyterians
By 1721, Presbyterians in Bere Regis were meeting at the home of Mary Batrix, a widow.

1721–22: Stone Work on Bere Church
Major stone work was carried out on Bere church during this year. The wardens' accounts show a total of £17.17s.10d., which included part of the mason's bill being £11.6s., and carriage of the stone from Purbeck. Entertaining the stone cutters included 2s.8d. 'when we made ye bargain with them'. David

Compton provided a new bell wheel for 14s. and a similar amount for other work. The ringers were given 7s.6d 'when the Bishop was here'.

1723: Gould Family Notebook
The Gould Family Notebook was begun by the family who lived on Woodbury Hill. It is mostly an account book and notebook of a builder and carpenter and deals mainly with the erection of 'standings' and 'bowers' for the Fair. Details of family matters such as births, marriages and deaths are interspersed with local events and regular comments on the weather. One of the first entries in the Gould Family Notebook recorded that '10 houses burnt at woodburyhill in ye yeare 1723'. Another early note was perhaps to help in the preparation for a possible confrontation: 'Memorandum – I do intend if god willing ye 3 day of ye fair to go to she for my mony for I do belive she has paid me severall bad peces of mony.'

1723–24: Rebuilding Work on Church
The church rate income for this year was £55.5s.4d. and covered the costs of two major projects. The first was the re-gravelling of the paths in the churchyard. Chalk foundations then gravel surfaces involved many loads of materials and Henry Phelps was in charge of the work. The total cost was £6.15s. The second major work was rebuilding and involved scaffolding for upper-level work. Some 55 bushels of lime (£1.7s.6d.), nine bushels of hair (6s.) and 500 bricks (5s.6d.) were the main materials, while James Lockyer and Henry Porter carried out the work for a total of £5.2s.2d. In addition £1 was paid for 1,000 'pears'.

Other sums for the year included: New clapper for the great bell (£2.12s.8d.), Mr Boyes for cleaning the clock for two years (15s.), David Compton for the church gate (£1.19s.6d.), Benjamin Moores for glazing and painting the glass (£2.4s.) and expenses 'For the woman that died at Lovelases' (The King's Arms) (10s.6d.).

1724: Poor Law Adjustment

A certificate of settlement under the Poor Law for John Lockyer alias Sexey at Bere Regis is now lodged at the Dorset County Museum, Dorchester.

1725: New Bere Vicar

Henry Fisher (MA, Balliol College, Oxford) was instituted vicar of Bere Regis on 19 November 1725. He married Mrs Susanna Williams at Bere on 1 November 1726. She was buried on 2 December 1757. He was vicar of Bere Regis for almost 48 years and during this time he made a table from a yew tree which is reputed to have grown in the churchyard. This table is still in use in the vestry and its legs are shaped like those of a horse. There was a small brass memorial to him (stolen in 1981) on the north wall of the north aisle depicting a skull and hour-glass, said to be symbols of mortality, and inscribed *Verbum non amplius – Fisher* ('The word and no more – Fisher'). Mr Fisher paid for the building of a detached part of Balliol College, Oxford, with the donation of £3,000. Details of the donation were reproduced as letters printed in Hutchins's *History of Dorset,* second edition (1796–1815) from the Revd Charles Godwyn to Hutchins and dated 14 August and 30 October 1767. Fisher died on 20 June 1773 aged 90.

1725: Southbrook Bridge

The ford across the Bere Stream at Southbrook was supplemented by a brick bridge in about 1725. This was rebuilt in 1806 and remained in place for a further century and a half. The ford also continued to be in use, not only as a crossing point but for abstraction of the crystal-clear water, in buckets for personal purposes and by horse-drawn water wagons for agricultural and building work.

1725–26: Thunder, Hailstorm and Fire

At least 56 men passed through the village who had been 'taken by Pirates' or 'taken by the Turks'. They were all given from 3d. to just over 1d. depending on whether they were travelling singly or as a group. The biggest group was 14 men who received 1s.6d. The churchwardens' accounts also show that 2s. were paid for a booklet on avoiding fire by lightning strikes. There are three payments to travellers who had lost by thunder, hailstorm and fire. They received 6d., 3d. and 9d. respectively.

Major wood work was carried out early in 1726 and included buying '4 tuns and 6 foot' of timber from Jasper Shetler for £10.2s.6d., while its transport from Whitchampton and the Blackmoor Vale cost an additional £1.10s.

1727: Little Tower Repairs

Building work continued on the church through 1727 and the churchwardens' accounts describe the location; 'the little Tower' probably refers to the east end of the north aisle being re-roofed again. The plumber also laid new lead on the roof. The whole job cost £9.19s.6d. An additional sum of £13.4s.8d. was paid to Mr Ham as half his bill for lead work around the church. The date of the payments is recorded for the first time by the wardens John Hewitt and William Talbott both of whom seemed to have some experience of trade accounting. The little tower work was mainly paid for in July and August. On 30 January Mr Tollerville was paid 3s.6d. for a rope for the third bell, then on 19 August he received 7s. for two more ropes.

Extraordinary celebrations for the crowning of King George II are shown in a payment on 14 August of £2.2s.8d. Some work involving carpenters seems to have suffered from insufficient preparation as Thomas Applin was sent to Cranborne 'to forbid the carpenters coming, ye timbers being not fetch't.' Benjamin Moores was paid £2.5s for painting the church walls (with scenes) and for the ladders that he needed. Lord Walpoole's servant was paid a shilling for a fox head. Payments for vermin during recent years was very extensive.

1728: Bell Support Breaks

The process of ejecting undesirable elements from the village is illustrated by an entry in the churchwardens' accounts. 'Horsehire and expenses in going to the Justice with three men warned out of the parish' had cost 2s.8d. William Gould and Thomas Applin were paid 3s. for taking up the third bell and mending the gudgeons and clapper. More seriously; the Great Bell had to come down then be put back after the stock broke and for this Edward Battrick also helped. The three charged 7s. A charge of 12s. was paid 'for putting Rebekah Meering into Court'.

1729–30: Vermin Extermination

George Young was the tax collector for the Church Rate in 1729–30 and for this duty he charged 4s.6d, while spending for the year totalled £48.16s.11d. One of the wardens for his year lived at Bere Heath and most of his expenditure of £2.6s.0½d was for the extermination of vermin.

Re-boarding and tiling the church porch cost a total of £1.3s.6d. while Thomas Applin was paid 15s.10d.

Junction of tunnels found under Court Green Farm in August 1981.

for iron work around the building. Additional gaol money of 18s.8d. was paid for the pennance of Aaron Burt's daughter Elizabeth, although the accounts do not detail for what. A new mat for the minister to stand on cost 6d.

1732: Church Seats Repaired

Major work on repairing the seats in the church cost 15s.11d. according to the churchwardens' accounts for 1732. Also one of many payments to travellers included 'Mr Browning who lost by Fire £500 (well attested): 6d.' in June. In December 'a man that had been taken into Algiers & used very cruely: 6d.' The warden on Bere Heath paid out £1.2s.7½d. for vermin heads.

1733: Morton-Pleydells Reserve Seats

A memorandum dated 31 May 1733 is preserved in the churchwardens account book:

At a Parish Meeting then held for the Parish of Beer Regis, it was agreed that the upper Seat in the Body of the Church next to Chancel is the Right and Estate of Edmond Morton-Pleydell Esqr as Owner of Shitterton Farm, And the two Lower Seats, save One, is the Property also of the said Edmond Morton-Pleydell, That the lower Seat in the same Isle shall be always in the right of the Vicar of this Place and his Successors for the time being. And it is agreed and ordered that the Lower Seat in the South West Corner of the Church shall be for the use of Mr Williams's Charity Boys and Schoolmaster for the time being, Witness our hands.

It was signed by the vicar and wardens.

1733: Ringers' Money Stops

Another memorandum is preserved in the churchwardens' accounts and is dated 24 December 1733:

At a Vestry then held of which Notice was given before, It was resolved & agreed That no Churchwarden of Beere Rs shall at any time hereafter pay any of the parish moneys for ringing of the Bells at any time whatsoever Witness our hands.

This is signed by the vicar and wardens. This seemingly draconian order was not adhered to, as by the next year the following memorandum dated 21 October 1734 appears:

It is agreed by us at this Vestry whose names are under written that the Churchwardens shall pay such Money for Ringing upon such Days as it hath been paid before Witness our hands.

1734: Payments for Vermin Heads Stopped

Payments for the destruction of vermin ceased during 1734. The churchwardens paid those who presented them with the heads of foxes, badgers,

otters, hedgehogs, polecats, stoats and sparrows (by the dozen). A fox was worth a shilling, while the others would yield a few pennies. Between 1612 and 1734 many thousands of birds and animals were destroyed, but there is no information of where the heads were buried.

There was another Great Storm during the year and church repairs included re-glazing windows, mending parts of the tower and tidying up the walls especially on the east side where plastering with lime and hair took place. The work cost £3.7s.9d., beginning with payments on 10 February 1734. In May the wardens paid the painter £4 for writing and painting the inside walls, while 1s.6d. was paid for a large brush for the church. Sixpence was paid to Thomas Applin 'for killing the sparrow & other work'.

1735: Henry Drax Refuses to Pay Rate

Henry Drax appears for the first time on the church rate list. He refused to pay his 12s. until the 28 June 1736 audit of the churchwardens' accounts. A statement by the wardens of June 1736 was later blotted out with ink after they had second thoughts:

This Blot proceeded from a Mem.dum intended for the use of the parish; but upon due reflection, eras'd, as not proper for the publick inspection. Edm Morton-Pleydell.

Some words are still discernable:

June ye...... the above date with...... relation to the...... by Mr Drax as a...... by the year from the...... of the...... as appears...... from the Deans Court...... Offices of the P...... ...... latter and of the book...... the parish by Mr Turberville...... have us over rul'd by the same...... Pleydell.

1736: Last Nine-Dozen Sparrow Heads

Despite the end of paying for vermin heads, churchwarden Mr Gould paid for nine-dozen sparrow heads (1s.6d.) by mistake but it was allowed to pass as he hadn't been told. Also from the warden's accounts, some 4s. were paid for the churchyard stile and William Welch was paid 1s.8d. for mending the window bars. More repairs to the porch involved £1.3s. for tiles and work. The figures were audited on 10 August 1737.

1737: Common Prayer Book Altered

Spending by the churchwardens had fallen to about a third of the sums being raised just 15 years previously. The income for 1737 was £17.17s.9½d. and the biggest expense was for tiling the porch again. This came to 19s.7d., while 'Painting ye Dial' cost 2s.6d. One shilling was paid for a pamphlet of instructions to alter the Common Prayer Book.

1738: Porch Floor Tiled

The church porch seems to have been finished by

1738 and the churchwardens' accounts show that the floor was the last main job to be completed. James Burges was paid 12s. for 600 paving bricks. Henry Potter and his son were paid £4.16s.10d. for plastering the church and used 120 bushels of lime, ten bushels of white hair and 9½ bushels of black hair for a total of £2.19s.9d. Benjamin Moores helped Mr Porter for eight days at a shilling per day. He was also paid 4s. for cleaning and oiling the Apostles. The pathways were also worked on again, by Henry Phelps who was paid 16s.

1739: New Belfry Floor

The churchwardens' accounts show that the belfry floor used 125ft of boarding, costing 16s.4d. and Mr Compton was paid 6s.8d. for laying it. Henry Porter and his son did work on the east end of the church during nine days which cost 13s.6d. for himself and 3s.9d. for his son. The ringers were paid a shilling when news came that Admiral Vernon had taken Carthegena. The claim had been somewhat exaggerated. At this time of excessive gin drinking, Admiral Vernon had, however, decided to dilute Navy rum which was from then on called 'grog' this being Vernon's nick-name. The 1739 figures were audited on 13 August 1740.

1740: Prayers at a Time of War

This is the last year for which churchwardens' accounts survive. It records the purchase of a new Common Prayer Book for the minister, which cost 17s.6d. and also a shilling was spent on a pamphlet containing a 'Prayer to be Read during Time of War'.

Work on the churchyard wall cost 12s.3d. and used 200 bricks, sand, four bushels of lime and half a pack of white hair. The audit for this year was made on 29 July 1741. The church rate ceased being compulsory in 1868 and stopped completely in 1929.

1740: County Divisions

The County Divisions were rearranged to form nine, these being Dorchester, Bridport or Beaminster, Blandford North (called Blandford), Blandford South (called Wareham), Shafston East (called Wimborne), Shafston West (called Shaftesbury), Sherborne, Sturminster and Cerne. Bere Regis was in the Wareham Division. The tything, taxation, care for the poor and many other matters were dealt with by officers responsible for their own division. The assessment for the county rate in 1740 was: Beer Regis (£3.3s.0d.), Hyde (7s.4d.), Kingshold (6s.0d.) and Shitterton (9s.1½d.).

1740: Bere Anabaptists

The dwelling-house in Bere of 'Grace Pitman, Anabaptist' was licensed for worship from 1740 to 1773. John Waldron was the Congregational minister in the village from 1746 to 1760 when he was replaced by Matthew Jackson. In the time of pastor David Jones, from 1769 to 1773, it was recorded that 'the number of hearers in the forenoon does not exceed 50 on an average, and in the afternoon from 120 to 140'.

1740: Woodburytide

Bere Regis churchwardens' accounts for the post-Puritan age – covering the years from 1682 to 1740 – show that Woodbury Hill Fair had grown into a five-day event. It now ran from 18 to 22 September each year. 'Woodburytide', as the locals knew it, was a calendar event across Dorset and beyond. It included St Matthew's Day and spanned the autumn equinox, with the sun crossing the equator, to herald the northern winter. By this time, many, if not most Dorset farm labourers were being given a day off to attend 'Woodburytide'. Dorchester, the county town, 'used to be practically deserted for the week of the fair'.

For the week before, vast flocks totalling upwards of 10,000 sheep, were herded towards Bere from the Dorset Downs and Cranborne Chase. As it grew in popularity the timetable of events unfolded into a class-linked structure. The original 'Wholesale Day', offering just about everything from haberdashery to hops, was followed by 'Gentlefolks' Day', which embraced the more stylish forms of entertainment and gaming, and was accompanied by a mass consumption of oysters. One of the later entertainments on this day was shaking country lads into new leather breeches by a breeches maker of Puddletown (a Mr Rolls).

Business was impossibly hectic in the single permanent hostelry on the hilltop and a number of traders,

No. 16 Blind Street as it was in 1970.

Buttressed brick barn at Philliols Farm dates to 1748.

Brick and timber cart shed south of Court farmhouse. Dating from the mid-eighteenth century, the roof timbers are believed to be from a shipwreck.

Bere Heath farmhouse dates from the eighteenth century.

Old Mill and No. 120 Doddings dates from the eighteenth century.

and most of the houses (some serving the beer through a 'hole in the wall') took out special liquor licences for the duration of the fair. 'Allfolks' Day' followed with a widening of the clientele and the arrival of more bucolic entertainments. All such events, from boxing and cudgel contests through to cock and dog-fights, were associated with rampant gambling. 'Sheepfair Day' was next, and a reminder that these were the county's staple stock, notable for its own breeds on the Dorset Downs and the insular Portland peninsula. Large numbers of cattle, oxen, horses and other live-stock were also stockaded for auction or private sale on the hill. Finally came 'Pack and Penny Day' as the

stalls were cleared (the pack element of the name) and remaining produce and products sold at bargain prices (a penny if you were lucky).

1741: Poor House at the Warren
The parish Poor House was built on Warren Heath, before 1741, on a site which Barbara Kerr indentifies in *Bound to the Soil* as being inside the angle of the 'unexpected and marked bend' in Warren Road between Warren hamlet and Warren House. By 1749 it had been refurbished and the village's 14 trades-men involved in the beer and ale business were supplying it through the poor rate. Payment records exist for 1741 to 1778.

1742: Naughty Boys on Woodbury Hill
The Gould Family Notebook records some sort of feud:

1742 July ye 25 being St James day Sunday will Ruttor John Baskome James harice broke ye window. Strangmans window 10 or 12 quarels about 4 a clock or 5 a Clock in ye afternoon Will Rutter ofered harice to give him a 2 to break our windo.

1745: Wet January to March
Weather as reported in the Gould Family Notebook: 'Memorandum in ye yeare 1745 it was a very wet winter & a very wet March I do not mind of ye like wet almost every day.'

1746: Pub on Woodbury Hill
A new pub was built on Woodbury Hill in July 1746. At the time of building, by Burgesses a local firm, the name had not been decided. It would be either The Sailor or The Taphouse. It was built in just seven days and according to the Gould Family Note Book took up 11 bushels of lime (88 gallons), had walls 10ft high and 13ft at the ends. Having a dedicated pub on Woodbury Hill during the Fair would have been a sound proposition as during Woodburytide such an establishment could earn as much as a pub in the village for a whole year.

1747: Local Elections
Borough of Wareham election. Candidates (and votes) were Henry Drax (257), Thomas Drax (205) Mr I. Pitt (192).

1748: Sheep Grazing at Bere
An inter-family contract is recorded in the Gould Family Notebook: 'An account between my son John & I 1748 he came with ye sheep into Bere fields ye 7 of Sept & went away ye first of October= so theare is 8 weeks diet at 3s. a week – 01=4=0.'

1749: Traditional Remedies
From the Gould Family Notebook: '1749 we botled our beer July ye 29'. Also the same year a remedy for sore skin; 'An exelent Recipei to make salve – take

Lard & beeswax & rosan & stur in some venis turpentine & yt will make a very good salve,' and 'to sumple any Joynts or fingers take ye Oyle of Saint Johns worth & anoynt ye greived place.' It seems that the writer had obtained a new book, 'The herbery is called ye *English Physician* & do give account of all maner of herbs.' Also, from the book, 'theare is a Stone cald a Coastick tuch a sorlip a present remidy.' In the same year, '1749 August ye 5 I soed Leekseed.'

1750: Ibernium at Bere?

Antiquarian research was imposed on Bere Regis, if inaccurately and inconclusively, with the claim by William Stukeley (1687–1765) that Woodbury Hill was the Ibernium of the Romans. The name comes down to us from the British section of a late-seventh-century list known as the Ravenna Cosmography. Stukeley decided that 'this verily is our Bere... where a yearly fair is kept'. His identification of Woodbury as being Roman was in keeping with the archaeological assumptions of the time in which earthworks were variously attributed to the British, Romans or Danes depending upon their shape. That on Woodbury Hill, being squarish, was thought to be Roman rather than Iron Age. This Latin place-name from antiquity – *Ibernio* meaning 'yew tree place' – is now associated with the River Iwerne and its villages. It seems credible that it took its name from the Roman fort inside the Iron Age ramparts of Hod Hill, north of Blandford. Unknown to most writers on the subject, there is even living evidence, as Dorset's only ancient yew wood still grows on the opposite slope.

1750: Beating the Bounds

From the Gould Family Notebook there is an account of the beating of the bounds of both Bere Regis people and those from Bloxworth:

Memorandum Concerning June ye 6=1750 Beer Folks & bloxworth people went a bounding together into ye east coman – we began at ye ditch between new close & beerhambrech ye first Stone is by a horning bush by ye way side: the next stone is in ye medle of ye pond: ye next is by a hirny bush about 100 or a 100 & 20 yard: ye next Stone is by ye way side to ye left of ye way about a 100 or a 100 & 20 yard: ye next stons are about a 100 or a 100 & 20 asunder theare are 2 stones about 16 yard asunder one west and ye other east to part hide and beer ye east is to part bloxworth and beer. then we goes down to the hedes corner and from yt thear is oak tree bouns a little ways from hide barn then from yt we goes to a oak tre in glasburys hedge & from thence we goe us ye hill & Thear 2 holes & when we are a top of ye hill we goes on to thomas hardys Grave and from thence we goe on to Boventon stone by Dorchester way: & from yt to a litle pond upon ye left hand of ye way coming from boventon stone: & behether yt is a nother pond in ye medle is a bound stone & from yt about 80 or a 100 yard is another bound stone.

Engraving of Bere manor-house on Court Green as seen by Hutchins's third edition, 1861, based on an older drawing.

The White House dating from the eighteenth century on Bowcroft Hill.

Interior of the brick cart shed south of Court farmhouse.

The two cottages on the west edge of Woodbury Hill, Nos 106 and 107, as pictured in 1970. They were demolished in 1980.

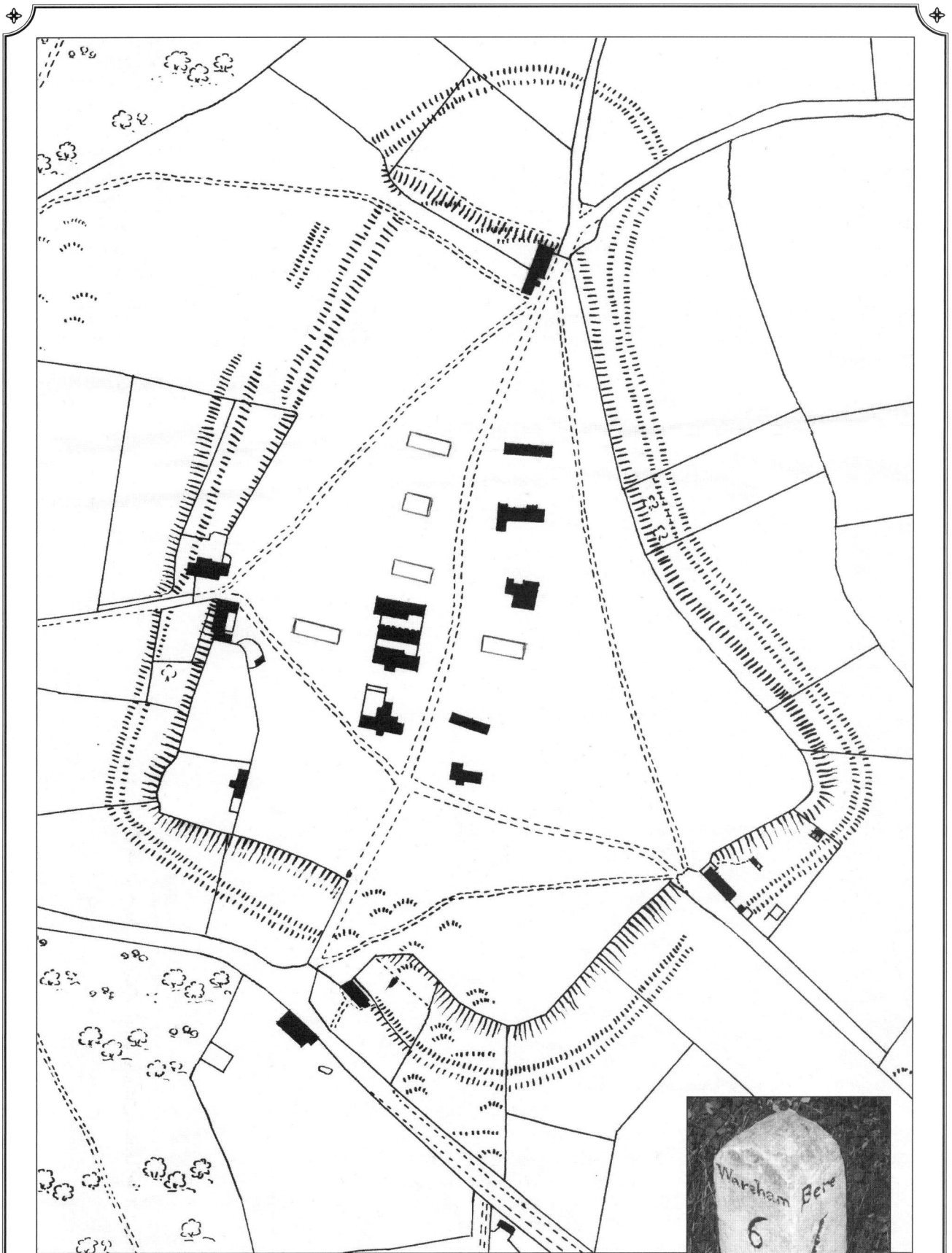

A 1902 map of Woodbury Hill showing buildings present then. The buildings in outline are those that existed in 1777.

Right: Milestones were placed on roadsides from the turnpike days of 1765.

1751: Wet March and Spring
According to the Gould Family Notebook, which was started in 1723, '1751 it was a terable wet march & springe.'

1752: 11 Days Missing
Cumulative errors in the Julian Calendar, set out by Julius Caesar in 45BC, resulted in the adoption of the Gregorian Calendar, which had been in use in Catholic countries of Europe since 1582. The day after 2 September became 14 September, and many believed that they had lost 11 days of their lives. Confusion, panic and anger resulted in some parts of the country but the effects locally seem to be limited to there being no baptisms, marriages or burials recorded in the parish registers during those eleven days in September 1752.

1758: Button Making at Peak
The grandson of Abraham Case died and was succeeded by Peter Case in the wire-button-making business that had been established in Bere Regis. The business operated out of No. 88 West Street; the best and most extensive premises in the place. Abraham Case had set up the business in about 1730–40 and the business grew to such proportions that huge profits were derived. At this time the main depot was at Milborne, with others at Piddletrenthide, Hanley, Woolbridge, Langton Matravers, Iwerne and Shaftesbury.

1762: Taxing Daylight
There are today some houses in Bere Regis where some of the windows are bricked up. This action dates back to a Parliamentary Act which came into force on 16 March 1762 and was popularly known as the 'window tax'. The regulations were that:

... every inhabited house containing eight or nine windows, and no more, shall pay 1s. each; for ten or eleven windows, and no more, an additional duty of 6d. each; for twelve, thirteen or fourteen windows, and no more, an additional duty of a shilling each; for fifteen, sixteen, seventeen, eighteen or nineteen windows, and no more, an additional duty of 3d. each.

Within weeks of enforcement there was total confusion at the randomly sliding scale of taxation, but many windows were sealed so that the lower rates could be paid.

1765: Wareham Turnpike Road
The first coach road into Bere Regis was a cul-de-sac, off a turnpike built across heathland north-west of Wareham, built by the Wareham Turnpike Trust in 1765–66. This took a direct line through Coldharbour, and across Sugar Hill, as it climbed towards the famous fairground on Woodbury Hill. From here it made a final twist, westwards and downwards, into Town's End where it joined North Street and entered the village. Its milestones survive in hedgerows and verges with the final two in the last mile (of a total length of 11 miles 16 poles) having been bypassed by later highways. Although now surfaced with tarmac, this length otherwise remains a perfect example of turnpike road-making.

By law, each able-bodied man had to give six days' labour on road work per year (or the equivalent in cash). The use of unspecialised labour meant that the work was badly managed and there were often shortages of materials, but the main benefits of the scheme were that the land was reserved for the road rather than it being used for agriculture and the old track ways remained in use. Roads became the responsibility of county councils from 1889 by which time many of the Turnpike Trusts had already become insolvent due to lack of revenue from tolls.

1766: Milborne Stays with Bere
At the Easter Sessions of the County Division it was noted that Milborne Stileham, while part of the Bere Regis Hundred in the Wareham Division, had no separate officers, so would remain part of Bere. By this time, however, it was maintaining its own poor. The population of this southern part of what is now Milborne St Andrew was 313 from the 1831 census.

1767: Kitcatt Family
Licensee James Kitcatt of the Drax Arms was born in about 1730, married in 1767, and died in 1818. He had come to Bere Regis as a child, with his widowed mother, and the family tradition was that they were Norwegians who had been shipwrecked on the Dorset coast. The villagers gave them a home and their name. This, in its English version, had been coined by the Kit-Cat Club of Protestant pamphleteers who met in London at the Cat and Fiddle, near Temple Bar, from 1703 to 1733. The tavern was kept by mutton pieman Christopher Cat. James Kitcatt was Nonconformist and married Mary Sergeant in 1767.

They ran both the Drax Arms (from 1777) and a farm in the parish. Their children were Cicely (1768), Elizabeth (1770), Emme (1771), Mary (1772), George (1774), James (1777), Anne (1778), John (1781), Charlotte (1784) and Thomas (1786). The middle son, James, succeeded his father as publican. Orthodox elder son George left the village for London in July 1790 after a rift over religion. He was apprenticed to red-haired bookbinder John Lovejoy of Dean Street, off Fetter Lane, and on coming out of his apprenticeship dropped the last letter of his family name, to adopt the standard spelling of Kitcat. He married and set up business as a master bookbinder in 1798, at No. 7 Bull and Mouth Street, which was on the site of the Post Office at St Martin's-le-Grand. Later he became an art master, at Bridewell Hospital, in 1809, and established a bindery there.

John Kitcatt, the third and youngest son of the

Cob and thatch barn where Southbrook becomes Rye Hill, shown in 1955. Southbrook Barn was demolished in 1972.

original James Kitcatt at the Drax Arms, also achieved some notoriety. He became a dissident preacher and settled in Newbury.

Another who left the village to espouse a cause was John Clench who made his move in 1787 and proceeded to pioneer the Sunday school movement. On his death, in 1821, he left the then substantial sum of £1,000 which enabled his sons George and James to establish themselves as G. and J. Kitcat, Bookbinders, at No. 22 Bartlett's Buildings, Holborn. The business survived into the late-twentieth century, having moved south of the river, to a works between railway arches in Shand Street and the approach to Tower Bridge.

1767: Serious Fire in Bere

There are reports of a serious fire in Bere Regis on 21 June 1767. There are few details as these events were common amongst thatched buildings. Although open fires were normal, it was usually strong or unpredicted winds that contributed to thatch catching fire in the summer.

Meanwhile, at about this time, the popularity of Woodbury Hill Fair was in decline. It was noted that in the 40 years since 1730 entrance tolls were only half of what they had been.

1770: Drax Arms Pub

The Drax Arms (or 'Drax's Arms') was so named from about 1770, formerly being The King's Head but locally 'Meerings'. Henry Drax had bought the estate formerly belonging to the Turbervilles in 1733. James Kitcatt was the tenant from 1777. From 1842 onwards Hall & Woodhouse of Blandford owned the pub.

1773: New Vicar for Bere

Thomas Williams was instituted vicar of Bere Regis on 4 December 1773 and resigned in 1817. He made a gift of the silver flagon to the church plate. It is about 6.5ins wide at the base and 4ins wide at the top where a hinged cover is fitted. The height is 10.75ins. It is used as a container for more wine during well attended Holy Communion services. The base has the following inscription: 'The Gift of Revd Thos Williams A.M. Vicar of this Parish 25th Decr 1812.'

1774: Hutchins' History

According to Hutchins' *History of Dorset* the name of the village is derived from the Saxon *byri* or *byrig*, hence Bere or Bery, meaning a habitation.

1784: Attempt to Seize A Quarter of Bere

A quarter of the manor of Bere was included in an extensive Deed with the demandee John Francklin, gent., against John Forster, gent., also for the transfer of lands and properties near Wimborne, Winterborne Zelstone and totalling 2,940 acres. Sir William Thomas was the vouchee.

1786: Depiction of Manor-House

An ink-and-wash drawing by J.B. Knight was made of 'Court House' at Bere. He chose for his view the east side of the manor-house, looking towards the church. This was at a time when the Turbervilles' house was still complete.

1788: The Fire of Bere Regis

The most serious fire broke out in Bere Regis between midnight and 1.00a.m. on Wednesday 4 June 1788 in The Crown public house. The fire spread rapidly to reach the vicarage and more than 40 other houses together with stables, barns and outbuildings. It was reported that the church was threatened several times but firemen and volunteers prevented any damage to the building. One of the consequences of the fire was that the parish records, stored at the vicarage, were lost completely. Only one person, a blind man, lost his life. The vicar and churchwardens made a newspaper appeal for assistance, while a periodical described the aftermath:

The scene of distress occasioned by this terrible conflagration is far beyond description. Many of the unhappy sufferers, who could not otherwise accommodate themselves, retired almost naked to the buildings erected for the fair on Woodbury Hill, where they found temporary shelter, and were very humanely and liberally supplied with every article necessary for their immediate relief, by the inhabitants of Blandford, Wareham and other neighbouring places.

Brick-buttressed barn at Woodlands, probably built in the 1780s.

renowned for her 'powers' with plants and their growth and this is why the vicar employed her. Four days after her arrival, Mr Ettrick's horse – a young and healthy animal – fell sick. At this point he made no connection, though looking back later, he did.

Susan Woodrow fell sick herself and left Turnerspuddle until June 1804. The day she came back the same horse cut its foot and was lame for more than ten days. Then on 2 September the horse caught a cold and the 'strangles'. It weakened catching other painful infections and died on 16 September. At this point Revd Ettrick firmly disbelieved in witchcraft and instead blamed the vet.

Four days later a pig fell ill and had to be killed, then the vicar's dog died unexpectedly. A horse that was borrowed to fetch potatoes became weak and was 'going the way of my horse by the vile witchcraft of a bad neighbour'. All the vicar's children became ill, the youngest very seriously and coincidentally Susan Woodrow acted as nurse at the birth on 22 July 1804. The child had never been well.

By November Mr Ettrick wrote in his journal, 'I was once incredulous about the power of witchcraft, but have no doubts remaining.' Of the child's illness, he writes: 'It is like a demoniacal possession and began immediately after the child was snatched out of the mother's arms, by a hag reputed to be a witch.' Finally after a dream, the vicar plucked up the courage and dismissed Susan Woodrow in January 1805.

Bridge at Southbrook pictured in about 1912.

1811: Census Figure
Village population from the census was 953.

1813: New Congregational Chapel
Despite John King's gift of a communion cup, Congregationalists in Bere were hardly gathering as one body during the Napoleonic Wars. They were split by a doctrinal difference over Arianism, whose adherents rejected the concept of the Trinity – comprising Father, Son and Holy Ghost – causing the two factions to hold rival meetings until they were eventually reconciled in 1820.

Meanwhile, thanks to a death-bed gift of £300 from benefactor King, they were able to build a new chapel which opened for worship, in Blind Street, in 1813.

1815: Property Values
The estimated annual value of real property in Bere Regis was £1,993, while the amount of rates to be raised for the poor was £834.

1816: Fire in Bere Regis
Another serious fire in Bere Regis occurred on 23 June 1816. Again there are few details but the time of year suggests that dried-out thatching was susceptible to the merest hot floating spark.

1817: Orator Henry Hunt
Postwar decline and distress started at Bere Regis with a disaster. A huge fire ravaged the village in 1817. It set the stage for new levels of misery, which nearly brought about a revolution in England, although postwar austerity took more than a decade to trigger demands for reform.

Agitation in Somerset, Dorset and Wiltshire was stirred by the 'radical reformer' Henry Hunt (1773–1835) of Manor Court, Glastonbury, who travelled the countryside and was nicknamed 'Orator Hunt'. This 'powerfully-made fellow' who looked like a butcher, spoke with impeccable loyalist credentials, as a member of the gentry who in 1801 had offered his entire £20,000 fortune to the government for the defence of the country, and to put himself and his servants into uniform. By 1810, however, he was in prison and sharing rooms with William Cobbett. In 1820, as a result of presiding over the 'unlawful meeting' in Manchester that we know as the Peterloo Massacre, he was imprisoned in Ilchester Gaol and exposed corruption and malpractice that were endemic in the judicial system. Hunt's non-party platform was for taking patronage out of ballots, introducing universal suffrage at a time when only the country's few freeholders could vote, promoting women's rights, curtailing royal honours, and repealing the corn laws. He unsuccessfully proposed in Parliament that all householders paying rates and taxes should have votes. Hunt had a rustic Dorset prodigy in Joseph Arch whose open-air meetings were recalled by Thomas Hardy.

1818: Bere's New Vicar
Carrington Ley is instituted vicar of Bere Regis in 1818 and died on 24 September 1864.

1818: Murder of Pregnant Woman
A Bere Regis woman, Priscilla Brown, was murdered on 14 May 1818. She had been about seven months pregnant according to Thomas Nott the Bere Regis surgeon who examined the body which had been found on a dunghill in Back Lane, behind West Street, Bere Regis. She had been suffocated. The father of her unborn child, John Gollop (who had recently married Charlotte Gilham) was arrested, tried, found guilty and hanged at Dorchester Gaol on 27 July 1818. The motive had been to avoid the possibility of having to pay maintenance money under a Bastardy Order. Priscilla Brown had already been receiving maintenance of 2s.0d. per week on account of her eight-year-old son by another man under a Bastardy Order.

1821: Census Figure
Village population from the census was 1,080.

1822: New Rules for Parish
An Act of Parliament was passed enforcing all parishes to display the name of the village at entrances, and stones were to be set up to mark parish boundaries. Also no lights from blacksmith's shops were to be visible from roads by night. Bonfires were prohibited within 80ft of the centre of a road. Straying cattle were to be impounded and 5s. paid for each beast for their return to its owner.

1823: Trade Directories
From 1823 to the Second World War, Trade Directories covering Dorset were issued. They include lists of gentry and trade persons and their area of business. Piggot & Co., Kelly's then the Post Office were the producers of most of these although occasional Directories were produced by others.

1824: Confirmation Service
According to the Gould Family Notebook: '1824 August 24 the Bishop Came to Bere and Confirmed A great Number of young Persons.'

1825: Harvest Time
Another entry in the Gould Family Notebook records: '1825 There was a great deal of wheat out by the 20 of July and the harvest was all most in by 24 of August.'

1826: Soldiers After Beer
Events on Woodbury Hill were recorded in the Gould Family Notebook: '1826 June ye 12 there were Some Horse Soldiers in Bere some of which Broke in to our House on Woodbury-hill where the Strong Beer were But The Officer put all Things Inn plase again.'

Also for the same year: 'In the year 1826 July 17 There were Wheat Cut Wheat Ricks Made By The 22 of July.'

1827: Manor-House Taken Down
By order of the Court of Chancery, all the lodges and nearly all the buildings at Court Green were taken down.

1828: Very Wet Weather
A weather report from the Gould Family Notebook: 'In the year 1828 A very wett Winter such as was not known by any man living before.'

1828: Methodist Chapel
The Methodists of Bere Regis built their own chapel down a small track opposite the Drax Arms public house in 1828. It was a barn/cottage-type building of wattle and was thatched. The dimensions: about 35ft (10.7m) long and 20ft (6m) wide. It was replaced by a brick and slate building in 1890 but was described as 'The First Wesleyan Church'.

1828: Food for the Poor
The Gould Family Notebook records: 'December 31 in the year 1828 was given at Bere an ox and half of Beef and eight Pounds worth of Bread given to the Poor of Bere The gift of Mr Sawbridge Esqr.'

1830: County Rearranged
Effective from 1 September, county divisions were rearranged for administrative purposes. These were: Dorchester, Bridport, Cerne, Wareham, Blandford, Wimborne, Shaftesbury, Sturminster and Sherborne. Bere Hundred came in two divisions, the Milborne Stileham part being in the Blandford Division, while Bere Regis, Kingsfold and Winterborne Kingston were in the Wareham Division. Milborne Stileham was already caring for its own poor, so beginning the separation from Bere Regis administratively. At this time there were seven borough towns sending members to parliament, where there had previously been just two. Also in Dorset there were 27 places other than Bere Regis where fairs were held, although markets were also called fairs at this time. A regular market was no longer functioning at Bere by 1830.

Areas in Bere Regis were as follows: Bugbarrow (hamlet), Chamberlain's Mill (farm and land), Dodding Beer (farm and land), Philiholds (farm and land), Hyde (farm, land and tithing), Kingshold (farm, land and tithing), Shitterton (tithing and hamlet), Snelford (hamlet), Stokesley (farm and land), Southbrook (hamlet), Culeaze (farm and land), Roke (farm and land) and Ryehill (hamlet, farm and land). After 1830 the Milborne Stileham portion of Bere Regis was transferred to the Blandford Division.

1830: Agricultural Riots
The year 1830 commenced with severe frost and snow, and the roads everywhere were completely blocked up.

the same meets Sherford Lake; thence eastward along the Sherford Lake to the point at which the same meets the boundary of the parish of East Morden, thence southward along the boundary of the parish of East Morden to the point at first described.

Despite this huge area, the number qualified to vote in the entire constituency only numbered 387. Two local landowners, from either side of the seat, considered their chances, and decided to stand for election for the newly formed Wareham seat at the first opportunity, on 13 December 1832.

The direct outcome of the riots was the establishment of the Dorset Yeomanry Cavalry, in two corps, for the eastern and western divisions of the county. Nationally, the problem was largely blamed on the Duke of Wellington's enervated Tory administration, leading to its replacement by a Whig Government. Some 700 people from around Blandford signed a petition calling on the county's Members of Parliament to support the Reform Bill in March 1831. The 'first' county MP, Edward Berkeley Portman did just that, but he was counter-balanced by the 'second' member, Henry Bankes of Kingston Hall [*Kingston Lacy*], who:

... assured the House that the inhabitants of Dorsetshire who were satisfied with the present constitution had refrained from presenting petitions, whereas the petitions which loaded the table were from dissatisfied persons.

A general election resulted. In the blue (Conservative) corner was John Hales Calcraft, the son of the late John Calcraft, of Rempstone Hall, who had the support of other significant landowners, including Revd Nathaniel Bond, Humphry Sturt and John Fyler. In the pink (Liberal) corner was eccentric squire John Samuel Wanley Sawbridge who had married Miss Jane Erle-Drax-Grosvenor in 1827, shortly before she inherited Charborough and Bere, and similar large estates in Wiltshire, Yorkshire, Wimbledon (where Admiral Drax later gave land to the Lawn Tennis Association, in recognition of which the family was granted a box) and Barbados.

When the result was declared there was a 'terrible row' which turned into a physical fight as Drax (140 votes) lost to Calcraft (175 votes) with 72 electors failing to go to the poll. It was a local victory for the cry 'Church and King versus Dissent'. Many saw reform as synonymous with revolution, but in reality it defused any such event, and far from their fears that 'the Sun of England's greatness had for ever set' the stage was ready for its Victorian expansion into the greatest empire the world had ever seen, across a quarter of the globe, with no further challenges to the constitution of Church or State for the rest of the century. Drax, it was reported:

... was of the opinion that his friends in the town of Wareham, *together with his numerous tenantry in Bere Regis and neighbourhood, would be sufficient to carry him into Parliament.*

1835: Gentlefolks' Day
The Revd Octavius Pickard-Cambridge reported seeing 20–40 gentlemen's carriages and turn-outs at Woodbury Hill Fair on Gentlefolks' Day (19 September).

1835: Church Alterations
In about this year the uneven and somewhat decayed pew seating in the church was replaced by new seats made from deal wood. Also a carved screen, which filled up the chancel archway with tracery similar to that of the roof, and some other ancient pews were removed. The floor of the nave, which was originally nearly 2ft below the level of the north aisle, was raised, which meant the old Norman pier columns were dwarfed and the proportions of the whole church were destroyed. This report was part of the descriptions told at the time of the restoration of 1875.

1838: Drax's Pagoda
Squire Drax's parkland pagoda at Charborough was damaged by lightning in 1838 and replaced by the 120ft Charborough Tower in 1839. 'For some reason the first question people usually ask about it is how many steps there are,' Admiral Drax wrote in his *History of Charborough*. 'The answer is 161 (including the wooden steps from the top floor to the roof).'

1840: New Turnpike Roads
Squire Drax sat for Wareham in the House of Commons for nearly half a century but infuriated his friends by changing allegiance from Whig to Tory. He also changed the road system. North Street and West Street became major highways after the Puddletown and Wimborne Turnpike Trust was incorporated through a private Act of Parliament in 1840. Squire Drax, as its sponsor, not only represented the borough of Wareham in Westmister, but was the owner of all that lay between Bere and Charborough Park, and much else beside and beyond. New roads were

Manor-house on Southbrook Road in 1930 was named by Mr Bedford whilst he lived there.

created with the biggest single batch of additions to Dorset's highways since the Roman Empire. They put Bere Regis on the map as the hub of an entirely new road system for central southern Dorset. The dynamic plan had six elements which were summarised for Rodney Legg by the late Professor Ronald Good, author of two works on *The Old Roads of Dorset*:

1. Wimborne (Julian's Bridge) – Lake Gates – Corfe Mullen.
2. Bere Regis (Royal Oak Inn) – Morden Park Corner – Lytchett Minster (St Clement's Inn; now Baker's Arms).
3. Almer link (Marsh Bridge – World's End).
4. Sturminster Marshall link (Newton Marsh, Newton Peveril – Creepers Lane – Bailie Corner).
5. Bere Regis (West Street) – Shitterton (bypassed) – Tolpuddle Ball – Tolpuddle – Burleston – Athelhampton – Puddletown (Ilsington House).
6. Bere Regis (Town's End) – White Post – Red Post – Winterborne Zelston (bypassed) – Marsh Bridge – Almer (bypassed) – Stag Gate – Lion Lodge – Henbury – Corfe Mullen.

The legacy and importance of these roads is that they and their successors hold modern trunk road status, as do sections of the strategic Folkestone to Honiton route (A35[T]) of the Second World War and its link to the postwar motorways (A31[T]). As for Drax's turnpike toll-roads, they barely enjoyed seven years before the sound of competition echoed across the Frome valley, as the railway arrived in Dorchester from Southampton and London, in 1847.

1841: Shitterton Girls' School
The earliest records of the school at Shitterton are those for 1841 when Ann Lockyer is noted as being the mistress from the 1841 census. The building at Shitterton had been rented from the Briantspuddle estate. There were about 18 headmistresses during the years that followed until closure in 1929, when the Rye Hill School opened.

1841: Drax's Wild Boar
By 1841 the 8,150-acre Bere Regis parish had a population of 1,394. As well as rearranging the road system, Squire Drax also reintroduced the now extinct British mammal which George Turberville had described – the wild boar – behind his long brick wall at Charborough Park. Pairs were brought from both Russia and France. The Russian breed, as one might expect, 'was wilder and more ferocious than the French'. Litters tended to run with their parents. Traditionally, for fattening, they were kept in what were called 'boar-franks', which explains a line in Shakespeare's Henry IV: 'Doth the old boar feed in the old frank?' Drax's animals lived in a much larger enclosure, until he had them caught in nets and moved to the 'new wilderness' he created, to the

south of the Poole road from Bere and Bloxworth, describing these locations in a letter to a friend:

I fenced them in [at Charborough] with a wood paling in the wood where I built the present tower, and used to shoot them. The latter part of the time I kept them at Morden Park, and bred a lot of them, feeding them on turnips and corn. They were savage and troublesome, however, to keep within bounds, and I therefore killed them. They were good eating when fed upon corn.

1844: Barrow Excavation
On 9 October 1844 gentlemen-archaeologists Messrs Shipp, Durden and others began excavating Bronze Age barrows on Bere Down. These are the notes generated by work on the first barrow:

The barrow is situated on a slope of gentle declivity and surrounded by the hill camps, Badbury, Flowers Barrow, the walled Bindon, on the chalk hills, and Milborne Rings. The position commands also a most extensive view of a series of barrows. Immediately contiguous, a few hundred yards to the south west, is a well-defined British earthwork, and about half a mile to the west of the latter may be seen the remains of a Roman villa.

The digging commenced by cutting a section, 6ft wide, on the south side of the mound, which was 10ft high, diameter of base 56ft, and 100ft in circumference. It was covered by a layer of earth and loose chalk. We had scarcely begun work when just under the turf, on the chalk, we found a small rude urn upon its side, filled with calcined bones. About 4ft from the centre, and 2ft deep, another urn was met with, inverted; this also contained bones. Some 4ft from it was a third urn, inverted, containing bones; a foot from it was urn No 2 inverted. On the south side of the barrow, and a foot from the last, we discovered a heap of ashes from 4 to 5ft in diameter, and 7 inches thick, evidently the site of a fire; underneath that layer was a circular cist, neatly cut in natural chalk, 3 inches thick.

About 5ft from the centre of the barrow, on the north side, and 3ft deep, three human skeletons were met with, lying at length, close together, feet to the east. The thigh bone of one had been fractured, and bore evidences of the most unskilful setting. These skeletons were in a high state of preservation, their skulls were intellectually proportioned, and every tooth in them perfect. We next cut a section transversely, east and west, about 8 feet wide and 4 feet deep. Twelve feet from the centre a large interment of calcined bones occurred, carefully placed together in a heap.

On the north-east side, nearly opposite, another cinerary urn was found. It was placed on a single layer of flints, and enclosed in a dry wall of a double course of large flints. This section was continued through without any further result. Our next step was to remove the greater portion of the remaining quarter; in the south-east and the south-west no

1870: Barrow Hill School Log Book

The log book of the Barrow Hill Boys' School began in 1870 and on 10 January the headmaster Mr John Stephens began work. There were 19 present. Work began on the playground on 25 January, then on 14 March girls from the Shitterton school were being taught in an adjacent house while alterations were being made to their school. The average attendance for the year March–March was 15 and about 30 for evening school. On 4 May work began on the new schoolroom which was opened on 26 September after the holidays. However, a holiday was given on 7 October to enable the workmen to finish the job. There was an exam on 8 December with 41 pupils present.

1871: Bere Missed the Train

Bere Regis's fortunes declined during the Great Depression that befell British agriculture during the closing decades of the nineteenth century. In 1871 the population was 1,366 but by the time of the 1891 census it had declined to 1,144. Much of the problem, as with Cerne Abbas in the heart of the Dorset Downs, was that Bere had missed the train in the era of railway building. Such locations experienced difficulties and distress from the cessation of coaching days until the coming of the car, which restored vitality to villages on main roads. The local turnpike roads lost their tolls and private status, becoming county-maintained highways, on 1 November 1873.

1871: Potato and Pea Picking

The Barrow Hill Boys' School log book reveals that a discovery was made on 13 March: that the previous headmaster was not certificated.

There were many absentees during 1871, in April potato planting reduced the numbers attending, while in July pea picking diminished the numbers. There was a 'choir treat' in July, then during the summer, harvesting caused many children to absent themselves. The autumn term was similarly affected by potato picking in October. From the register it is noted that there is a Robert Torreville attending.

1871: State of the Church

In August 1871 members of the British Archeological Association visited Bere Church and, although noting the inspiring ancient architecture, were somewhat critical of the state of the building and the fittings. The most alarming was that the columns and arches separating the north aisle were leaning outwards perilously. The walls had squalid dressings of whitewash, the box-pews and floor were rickety. The great west window had been bricked up for many years – tradition saying for the convenience of villagers who were given to the game of rackets. There were immense quantities of earth piled up against the walls outside, almost completely concealing the plinth at all places; the result of centuries of burials around the building. Inside, many fitments had the legible

graffiti in latin *cito peritura* or 'summon an expert'. A Restoration committee was set up consisting of the following: the Earl of Eldon, Mr Montague Guest, Mr Charles Hambro, Mr H. Williams, Mr C.J. Radclyffe junr, Mr N. Bond, Mr Arthur Mansel, Mr F. Lys, the vicar and the churchwardens.

1873: Restoration Work Begins

In March an engraving (based on a photo) of the church appeared on fund-raising brochures for the restoration. Work began on restoring the church in about November 1873. The architect was Mr George Edward Street RA, and his Clerk of Works was Mr Redden. The managing foreman was Mr Abley while the resident foreman was Mr Ham. Total cost was about £7,000 with £2,703 coming from subscriptions and donations and about £3,847 was donated by Mrs Egginton specifically for restoration of the chancel in memory of her mother who had died on 20 December 1853. A brass plate in the chancel details this gift, where there are also ten angels carved by Mr Harry Hems of Exeter, who also restored the figures in the nave roof.

The chancel was expertly painted by Mr D. Bell of Fitzroy Square, London. In the nave the figures in the roof were repainted to match colours that still remained on them. Whitewash around the church was replaced but when the old was removed it was found that most of the internal surfaces had once been extensively painted with scenes and figures. Pieces of tracery were found built into the walls,

Church interior in March 1873 before the restoration of the building. Points to note are the painting at the east end of the nave and the high box pews in the nave.

Workmen and scaffolding in the church during restoration work, c.1874.

Engraving of the church from the south-east, made in March 1873 for the cover of a fund-raising pamphlet.

removed and put back where they had been 300 years before. The nave and chancel roofs were covered with 'seven pound' lead. All this work was carried out by the contractors Messrs Hale & Son of Salisbury. At the time of the church opening on 7 October 1875 a sum of £450 was still owed by the parish.

1873: New Cemetery

There were 61 boys on the register at Barrow Hill Boys' School. Henry House was a pupil-teacher for the Fourth Year at this time. There was a holiday on Tuesday 24 October for all to attend the Consecration of the additional burial ground at Cemetery Lane, Bere Regis.

West Street, Bere Regis, in about 1873. The Post Office building was on the site where the lawn at the front of Cyril Wood Court is now located. The Post Office disappeared in 1902. At the door is Mrs Dowland the post mistress with Miss Eliza Lane, her assistant.

1873: The Horse and Jockey Pub

In about this year Bere Heath Farmhouse was in use as a public house. Its name was The Horse and Jockey and according to the trade directory for 1875 was being run by Mr Haggett and Mr Thomas. It is said to have been forcibly shut, probably in about 1878, as a result of a certain amount of unruly behaviour in the neighbourhood, for which the inn was considered responsible. The signboard of this inn is said to have survived with the Haggett family until the 1970s.

1873: Thomas Hardy at the Fair

Thomas Hardy visited Woodbury Hill Fair on 21 September during the course of his research for the novel *Far From The Madding Crowd*, published 1874.

1874: Scarlet Fever in Bere

Boys at the Barrow Hill School were able to attend evening classes, but these were mainly held in the winter months. The school inspector came to visit on 27 March and noted that there were 57 boys on the register. Pea picking caused considerable absence on 3 July 1874 and in September the school was closed for a week due to Woodbury Hill Fair. On 30 September there was a holiday in the afternoon as a bazaar was being held in aid of the Heath School Building Fund. An entry for 6 November states that scarlet fever was in the village.

1874: Radclyffe Portrait

Despite the economic downturn, the gentry had little difficulty raising more cash to pay for a portrait of a master of foxhounds than Bere's Nonconformists spent on building their schoolroom. The recipient of their largesse was Charles James Radclyffe at Hyde House, who was well respected in hunting circles, as this report from *Dorset Sporting Runs* confirms:

Bere Regis church in 1875 just after the completion of the restoration work and with newly-planted yew trees in the churchyard.

One of the principal social highlights of Dorset's hunting circles took place on 9 April 1874 when it was Charles Radclyffe's pleasant duty to receive a splendid portrait of himself and the pick of his pack of hounds. Those chosen to be so honoured were Lady-blush, Vengeance and Frantic in the front row, and behind them Dorcas, Laura, Watchful and Narrative. Mr Radclyffe's Hounds were painted by Stephen Pearce, as a commission funded by public subscription, which had raised £757.18s.0d. from 215 donors.

1875: Chamberlayne's School Opened
The new Bere Heath School at Chamberlayne's was opened for the first time on 11 January. The mistress was Miss Clara Martin, a second-year student from the Brighton Training College, with the assistant pupil-teacher Jane Galton who transferred from the Bere Regis Girls' School.

There were 46 children on the first day and by 1 February there were six more. By 4 March irregular attendance was already a problem and an entry in the log book for 30 June mentions haymaking being an excuse for absence. The autumn term began badly with absenteeism due to the harvest taking many boys away for work. There were two days' holiday on 21 and 22 September for Woodbury Hill Fair, while the school was closed on 7 October 1875 on account of the opening of Bere Regis church after the renovation.

1875: Acorn and Potato Picking
The Barrow Hill Boys' School log book records that on 5 February scarlet fever again broke out in the village. There were 54 boys present for an exam on 5

March and on 16 April 1875 there were 67 on the register. H.P. Tozer began as monitor on 14 May then on 2 July Henry Webb resigned as headmaster and was replaced on 5 July by William Bland Taylor who was certificated '1st Year 2nd Division'. There were 72 on the register at the beginning of the autumn term but there was absenteeism in November due to acorn and potato picking.

1875: State of Disrepair
Under the guidance of the vicar, the Revd Francis Warre, the church was repaired, enlarged and made good in many respects. Before the restoration was completed it was noted that:

... the soil had accumulated round the walls and the damp had seriously injured their stability; the magnif-icent roof was in a dangerous state of decay; the pillars and arches were clogged with many successive coats of whitewash; the interior was encumbered with high box-pews huddled together without any pretence at arrangement, which reached up to the spring of the arches and concealed the carving of the capitals; the moulded timbers of the roof were the hiding places of innumerable bats, which used to emerge from their hiding places on dark Sunday afternoons to the delight of the boys, who swept them down with boughs of trees as they floated along ghostlike and dashed in the faces of the nodding congregation.

1875: Turberville Vault Opened
During the restoration work to the church, completed in 1875, some of the tombs were moved or repaired.

Part of the work included altering the floor levels and during this work in the south aisle the floor slab sealing the Turberville vault was lifted for reseating. What the churchwardens found were steps down to racks of coffins on one side of the chamber. They made paper-rubbings of the plates that still existed on the coffins.

1875: New Church Bell
The third bell in the church tower has the following inscription: 'J. TAYLOR & Co. BELLFOUNDERS LOUGHBOROUGH 1875'.

1875: Restored Church Opened
Opening day of the restored church took place on 7 October 1875. In the village the streets were decked out with bunting and there were floral arches set up on many properties. The first service of the day was held at 11.00a.m. but the vicar had written to parishioners asking them not to go to this service; they would have their own service at 6.00p.m. It was a visitors-only service starting with a procession from the vicarage. The church was full with about 600 people. Chairs were added down the central passage of the nave and extra chairs were placed in the aisles. The Bishop gave the sermon then a collection of £109 was made. The service ended with Holy Communion.

A luncheon followed the service, this being held in a large marquee set up in the field west of the church, with catering by Mrs Dunn of the Junction Hotel, Dorchester. The numbers were far in excess of those expected and there were no second helpings. The vicar toasted the Bishop and reminded those present that they could approach the Bishop for advice at any time. The Bishop responded by saying that he did not enjoy these types of events in his younger days but was getting to like them as he got older. Secondly he stated that he hoped the practise of selling seats in the church would soon end. At 3.00p.m. there was a dinner for the workmen and labourers in the same marquee. There were about 250 present and the churchwardens, farmers and tradesmen of the village acted as carvers. Numbers were about twice that expected and servings were small. The vicar apologised for the small helpings, then said that he hoped they would not get drunk in the village later. The evening service for the parishioners was at 6.00p.m. and the church was filled with villagers. Their service was taken by the Revd E.M. Clements, vicar of Clifton and past curate of Bere Regis. He was assisted by the present curate Revd R.M. Hobson with Mr W. Smith from Wimborne Minster at the organ. The collection was £13.

1875: Church Window Scenes
The windows of the church had all been filled with stained glass, forming a continuous series of gospel history, designed and executed by Messrs Hardman of Birmingham, and paid for by Mrs Egginton, the lady of the manor and later Mrs Drax, to whose

munificence the restoration fund was largely indebted. The subjects of the windows are as follows:
The Great West Tower Window:
  The History of St John the Baptist
North aisle, west window: The Nativity
North side windows:
  1) The Miracle at Cana; Well at Samaria; Mount at Nazareth
  2) Call of Peter; Sermon on the Mount; Tempest Stilled
  3) Confession of St Peter; Transfiguration; Suffer Little Children to Come Unto Me
  4) Raising of Lazarus; Christ's Entry into Jerusalem; Cleansing of the Temple
East window of north aisle:
  Christ washing the Apostles' Feet; Last Supper; Crossing the Kedron
Chancel, north side:
  1) Gethsemane
  2) Pilate Washing his Hands
  3) Via Dolorosa
East window: Crucifiction.
Chancel, south side:
  1) Deposition
  2) Entombment
  3) Resurrection
South aisle, east window: Harpers on the Sea of Glass
South side windows:
  1) Heraldic with Turberville Coats of Arms
  2) St Michael Conquering Satan
  3) Heavenly Jerusalem
South aisle, west window:
  Salvation to God and the Lamb.

1876: Short Appointments
At the Bere Heath School a new monitor was installed on 29 March but was discharged after a month for incompetence and a new assistant teacher was appointed. The beginning of the autumn term saw a new mistress, Miss M.A. Pritchard, but she sent in her resignation on 24 November and left on 15 December. The usual absenteeism included that for potato and acorn picking mentioned on 13 October in the log book.

1876: Big Birds Shot
Sometime in 1876 the keeper at Hyde shot an osprey which was duly stuffed and added to 'Mr Radclyffe's collection'. That September an even more exotic visitor, a hoopoe, was 'picked up dead on Roger's Farm' at Bere Regis. Radclyffe rounded off a productive year by shooting a rare hybrid of a black grouse and pheasant for the Hyde House collection.

1876: Ceiling Falls Down
There were 66 on the register of Barrow Hill Boys' School but on 17 March only 27 turned up due to the foxhounds meeting in Bere Regis. By June both George Wellstead and Pitt Tozer were noted as being

Above: *Horse trade day at Woodbury Hill Fair, c.1880.*

Left: *Woodbury Hill Fair, c.1912, showing a variety of stalls and sideshows.*

the School Inspector came to visit, there were 57 present and the inspector said that this exceeded the numbers permissible in the schoolroom and classroom together, which could only be 52. On 9 December two children were sent to the Barrow Hill School.

1881: Stone Bridge
Chamberlayne's Bridge was rebuilt in stone by the county. In 1961 a stone was found among rubble from roadworks on the roadside verge at Worgret by Mr K. Stickley of Bere Regis, a DCC roadman. It bore the following inscription: 'CHAMBERLAINS BRIDGE, REBUILT 1881, WALTER J. FLETCHER, COUNTY SURVEYOR, WILLIAM HAMMETT, BUILDER.' The bridge suffered considerable damage from tanks during the Second World War and was replaced in 1956 by a reinforced concrete bridge with steel parapet rails.

1881: Census Update
The population of Bere Regis in 1881 was 1,284, excluding 248 persons living in the hamlet of Milborne Stileham who were at that time included in the parish. Its 885 acres have since been absorbed into adjoining Milborne St Andrew. The cemetery was extended further to the south during 1881.

1881: Birds on the Heath
Colonel Hambro, from Milton Abbey, shot a young green sandpiper at Bere Regis on 15 August 1881. John Clavell Mansel-Pleydell (1817–1902) of Whatcombe House also records in *The Birds of Dorsetshire*, published in 1888, that a male hen harrier 'frequented the neighbourhood of Bere Regis for several days in the early part of June 1887.' In 1875, another 'blue hawk' – as they used to be known – 'was procured at Hyde'.

Using the vague but definitely plural word 'others' he refers to specimens of Montagu's harrier that were shot on Bere Heath in 1871. Riding over 'Bere Field' in October 1884, Mansel-Pleydell saw a buzzard flying low over the stubble, which proceeded 'to pick up a partridge, which it held screaming in its claw'. As the Victorian naturalist and his companion headed to the rescue the predator dropped the prey which 'escaped unscathed'.

1882: Butt Lane School Transfers
As revealed in the Barrow Hill Boys' School log book, 1 February was a holiday on account of the consecration of the Burial Ground extension at Cemetery Lane. Then on 1 May the school was closed in the afternoon for the funeral of Miss White (mistress of the Girls' School at Shitterton) who died of diabetes after four days' illness. During the year there were several more admissions of boys from the Butt Lane British School. On 13 November Purchase's waxwork exhibition was in the village again. Some 48 boys sat for exams on 5 December.

1882: Village Photography
Walter Pouncey, photographer of 38 High West Street, Dorchester, photographed the church and surrounding areas, originally for the booklet *A Historical Sketch of Bere Regis, Dorset with Architectural Description of The Church of St John the Baptist*, by the Revd E. Venebles, M.A., Canon of Lincoln and Chaplain to the Bishop of London. It was printed by H. Spicer, County Printer.

1883: Sent Home for More Money
Until 1891 scholars attending school had to bring money with them, usually one penny per week. The log book of Barrow Hill Boys' School reveals that on 28 May 1883 three boys were sent home for not bringing the money. George House resigned as master on 13 July 1883 and William Dalton took over on Monday 16 July. Mr Dalton was taken seriously ill on 9 November, then Charles Hiscock took over on 27 November. Mr Dalton resigned on 21 December.

1884: Bonus for Good Attendance
The Barrow Hill Boys' School log book gives the dimensions of the schoolroom as 35ft 9ins long by 16ft 9ins wide, with height 13ft, while the classroom was 15ft long by 14ft wide and 10ft 6ins high. At a committee meeting on 26 May it was decided that the old fees paid by the boys at the beginning of each

week be kept as they are, but enforced more rigorously. Children of labourers would pay 2d. for the first child and 1d. for the second. Children of tradesmen or dairymen (but not journeymen) would pay 3d. for the first child and 2d. for the second, while farmers and others with a rental of £50 gross would pay 6d. for their first child and 3d. for the second. The increases went with a promise that the extra plus a 1s. bonus would be paid back if the child was present at both the exam and for three quarters of the days that the school was open for teaching. In July there were 48 on the register, and the new rules were enforced as the entry for 14 October 1884 states that a pupil had been sent home for the additional penny as he had only brought 2d. instead of 3d.

1884: One Foot in the Grave
One of the most bizarre burials in the cemetery at Bere Regis was the leg and foot of Charlie Tucker from Bournemouth. When Mr Tucker had an accident aged 18 at Bere Regis, his leg was buried there. He made his third visit to his grave in 1957 when aged 91.

View from Bere Regis cemetery in about 1918 with church and Methodist chapel in the background.

Inset: *Revd William Farrer, vicar of Bere Regis, 1886–99.*

1884: Problems Over New Fees
There is a note in the log book of Bere Heath School for 27 May regarding the fees payable by children each week. The infants did not have to pay, and the boys were to pay the same as at Barrow Hill School. Girls were to pay 1½d. as the first child of a family and another 1d. for the second girl. There was an extra penny to be paid by the eldest child which would be returned with a 1s. bonus if attendance was 75 per cent or greater. The result of the increase is illustrated by the entry for 9 June when 13 children were sent home for not bringing the extra money, while on 13 June there were many absentees due to the new fees.

A report dating from September 1884 was on the infants' teaching room. It was just 8ft square and was considered suitable for ten children only, but there were 18 on the books with average attendance being 16.3 infants.

1885: Back to Old School Fees
Average attendance at the Bere Heath School for the winter and the spring term was 30.9 and 32.6 respectively. The school fees were simplified from 27 September. The two eldest were to pay 2d. each per week per family and any other children were to pay 1d. per week. The 2d. fees were returnable at the end of each year for good attendance. There were 40 on the register later in the year.

1885: Beating the Bounds
The increased fees being imposed at Barrow Hill Boys' School were lowered to the previous level by 2 October, but those families with three or more children at the school had to pay a penny each instead of them being free if elder children from the same family were attending. Half of the 2d. fee was returned to families whose children had attended 75 per cent of days. There was considerable absence on 13 November when the parish 'beat the bounds'. This ceremony dated from many years past when parishioners would walk around the parish boundary to establish and maintain its extremities. The parish boundary is over 20 miles (32km) long.

1886: Grandmother Shot
The *Dorset County Chronicle* dated 14 October 1886 carried the following story:

SHOCKING MURDER AT BERE REGIS: A YOUNG MAN SHOOTING HIS GRANDMOTHER. Shortly before going to press, information reached us of a murder committed in this village. A young man named Sidney Russell, aged 21, on Tuesday night shot his grandmother, Sarah Scutt, aged 79, with a pistol. After committing the dreadful deed he went to the police station and gave himself into the custody of PC Bugby, to whom he confessed his crime, for which no motive has yet been assigned. When surrendering himself he said to the constable 'I have shot my grandmother; you must go and look into it.'

This was at five o'clock in the morning. The young man lived with his grandmother, with whom, it is said, he was not on very friendly terms. It is also stated that he was on the eve of going to Australia, and that his luggage had been taken to the station at Wareham. We hear that Russell formerly lived in Dorchester, where his father was a butcher [later found to be incorrect]. *The murdered woman was found lying on the floor of the room, dressed, so that it is most probable she had not been to bed* [not correct – she was in her night clothes].

1886: Inquest at School
From 26 March a new monitor was employed at the Bere Heath School at a shilling per week, to assist with the infants. On 17 May there were 57 on the register but 14 of them were absent. Miss Horth, the mistress, wrote in the log book for 15 October:

The Methodist chapel in Bere Regis pictured just after completion in 1890.

The river plain at Doddings looking east toward Bere Heath in 1890. This was before William Bedford built the cress beds at Doddings.

The water-wheel at Roke Farm pictured on 12 June 1984.

The present Roke Mill was built in 1890 and this photograph taken in June 1984 shows the water-wheel being refurbished.

White Lovington House, Bere Regis, pictured in 1970.

Drax Hall in North Street, pictured in May 1991, was converted in 1893 from a Congregational Church.

falling down, the odd ancient wall falling and rocking chairs starting to rock. The most severe effects include church bells ringing and chimneypots being thrown down, although a slight shaking is all that seemed to be felt in Bere Regis.

1889: Job Bugby New Head
On 9 August 1889 Charles Hiscock resigned as master of Barrow Hill Boys' School and on 16 September Job Bugby commenced duties as master. There were about 60 on the register. On 23 September the school closed for Woodbury Hill Fair, while between 2 and 30 December, the school was closed due to a diphtheria epidemic hitting the village. There were further diphtheria outbreaks in the winter and summer of 1890.

1890: Milborne Stileham Separates
From 2–30 December 1889, the schools had been closed due to an outbreak of diphtheria, and as the epidemic continued they were again closed in February 1890. Altogether seven children died from the disease in January and February, two families having suffered two deaths in each.

The winter was the third during which the village oil-lamps had been in use for street lighting.

In this year Milborne Stileham was separated ecclesiastically from this parish and joined to Milborne St Andrew. From before the time of the Domesday Survey (1086) the boundary between the Hundreds of Puddletown and Bere was marked by the Bere Stream, causing the village of Milborne to be divided, with the St Andrew portion in Puddletown Hundred and Stileham in Bere Hundred. Although there were many boundary changes over the centuries, it is remarkable that this early arrangement should have persisted at Milborne Stileham where some of the inhabitants, although only a few yards from Milborne St Andrew church, were Bere Regis parishioners with a church some 3 miles distant. By the nineteenth century, however, the people of Milborne Stileham were regarded for all practical purposes as parishioners of Milborne St Andrew, but there were many anomalies and the 1890 parish boundary revision was consequently welcomed by all concerned.

[Information taken from Bere Regis Parish Magazines]

1890: Chapel Rebuilt
A Methodist chapel was built on the site of the old one. There were two foundation-stones. The one in the NW corner was engraved: 'This Stone Was Laid By Revd J.T. Waddy B.A., April 28th 1890', while that on the south-west corner read: 'This Stone Was Laid By Mr D. Ballam C.C........ 1890'. The building was 37ft (11.3m) long and 23ft 6ins (7.2m) wide.

1890: Late Harvest
The Bere Heath School recorded that there were only 40 on the register on 21 March, seven having left to attend the Barrow Hill School, but this had risen to 53 by 11 July. These were composed of 22 girls and 31 boys. A log-book entry dated 1 August notes that 'Children are beginning to stay away in order to take their father's dinner to the harvest fields.'

1890: West Mill Fire
The old mill at the west end of the village was destroyed by fire in about 1890. A Parish Magazine of 1891 refers to it as 'the Burnt Mill'.

1891: Menagerie at Bere
After the longest and coldest winter for 50 years, a heavy snow storm occurred on 9 and 10 March, and the snow lay to an average depth of more than a foot with considerable drifting. Food became scarce as main roads were completely blocked, and some lanes were still 3–4ft under snow a fortnight later.

The 1891 census showed that the population of the parish had decreased from the 1881 figure of 1,284 to 1,144, and this was attributed to 'long continued agricultural depression'.

Bostocks' Menagerie visited Bere Regis on 7 September, when lions, tigers, wolves, elephants, camels, monkeys, and many other animals could be seen. November 5th was celebrated by a bonfire and a procession through the village led by the Bloxworth Band.

[Information taken from Bere Regis Parish Magazines]

1891: Snow Enters Schoolroom
Complaints about very cold weather were noted at Bere Heath School on 12 January. The mistress noted that: 'This room has no second ceiling, the rafters are exposed, so the wind comes in from all parts of the roof joinings; even snow and rain will find the way in...' In February there were 42 on the register and by 24 April the number had increased to 52.

1892: Sudden Crash During Service
There was panic in church at Evensong on Sunday 9 October when the vicar, towards the end of his sermon, had just quoted Tennyson's words 'the dead are not dead but alive'. Immediately, a 'tremendous crash was heard in the belfry, then a rumbling and a pause then another roar'. Members of the congregation, particularly those at the back, scrambled over one another in their haste to get to the door. The breaking of a 6cwt clock weight suspension cord, which had shortly before been wound to its full height, was found to have caused the disturbance. The weight, upon hitting the floor of the ringing chamber, had rebounded with such force that it had broken out through the 2ins thick wooden casing and finally knocked over a ladder. The incident served to recall a similar panic of some 50 years earlier (i.e. in about 1840) when a piece of masonry from the tower fell on the nave roof during a service. One woman is said to have hidden under the altar whilst other

members of the congregation jumped out of the box pews rather than use the doors.

[Information taken from Bere Regis Parish Magazines]

1892: First School Photograph for Six Years
Potato picking caused absences at the Bere Heath School on 21 October, but on 23 November the pupils were photographed at the school. There had not been a school photo taken since 1886.

1892: Vicar Shoots Rare Bird
An avian rarity, the Squacco heron, was observed on the Bere Stream in 1892 by Revd Octavius Pickard-Cambridge. He may have done more than merely look as the record is ambiguous and implies that he quite possibly shot the bird. The rector was an eminent naturalist, being a national expert on spiders, and also starred on the local stage. *The Rivals* was Bere's amateur theatre production, of 1895, in which Octavius Pickard-Cambridge took the part of Sir Anthony Absolute.

1892: Kennels for the Hunt
Mrs Ernle-Erle-Drax of Charborough Park erected the Kennels of the South Dorset Hunt in 1892, on downland north-west of White Post, a mile out of the village in sight of the road to Winterborne Kingston. A pack of 40 hounds was established and Monday, Thursday and Saturday selected for its days in the field.

1892: Steam Ploughs and Haulage
Charles Cobb who inherited 30 acres on Woodbury Hill from his father, Samuel Cobb, saw the potential of mechanisation. He saved up £250 and bought a steam-traction engine. Not only did it replace the horses – costing less in coal than they had eaten in corn – but it was available for hire. One of the most profitable contracts was to supply Bere's pure water from Southbrook, to the Army, which returned each summer to a tented encampment in the middle of dry heathland near Bovington Farm. Cobb fathered 17 children, of whom 12 were boys, and 10 became engine drivers. One of them, Charles Cobb junr, was killed in Cornwall while working there for Dorchester Steam Plough Works which had been established by Francis Eddison (1841–88). Having put the sheepleazes of the Dorset Downs under cultivation for grain it expanded operations across the whole south-western peninsula. Sidney Cobb recalled that on the land, locally, he and his brothers were the odd ones out:

We were a clan apart in a job peopled by Northerners. Eddison found his staff not in Weymouth but Wolverhampton. They were brought up there with boilers, batteries and belts. Apart from we, the average Dorset labourer was out of his mind with valves and pumps, and only knew chains and ropes. Us brothers

were the elite and that showed as we were never short of a sovereign. In father's case it soon found its way to the Drax. He was the life and soul of the village.

1892: Guy Fawkes Night
Guy Fawkes night was celebrated in the village. Hand bills noted that:

... the procession to convey the chariot of Mr Fawkes to the stake was to leave the Mill at seven o'clock, and shortly after the appointed time, the strains of the Bloxworth Band were heard, and the flaring torches of the enemies of poor Guy lit up the village streets. The quality of picturesque dresses of the chief executioners and their followers showed to great effect both in the march and around the bonfire. The bonfire was prepared in a field on the slope of Woodbury Hill. A very good selection of fireworks under the direction of Mr Hibbs were let off, whilst the bonfire was burning.

1893: Severe Gales in December
In June the parish clerk, Mr John Lane died, having held the office since 1875 on the death of his father William Lane, who had himself been clerk since 1840.

The fifth annual Flower Show attracted a record 500 entries.

A large Scots Fir on Rye Hill which had been a prominent landmark for many years, was blown down in a severe gale on 12 December.

[Information taken from Bere Regis Parish Magazines]

1893: Picking Acorns and Nuts
Absenteeism at Barrow Hill Boys' School, Bere Regis was noted particularly on 13 October 1893. The reason for absences was picking up acorns and nuts. Number on the register for the year averaged about 53 boys.

1893: Enlarging Infants' Room
It seems that the mistress at Bere Heath School made a formal complaint about the size of the classroom. The log book records her quoting Rule 7(a) of Schedule VII of the Code and that the infants' room was just 8ft by 10ft and it needed enlargement. The vicar and two school managers visited to discuss the enlargement on 7 July. The autumn term began on 11 September just when the workmen arrived to make the alterations by knocking down walls. 'Pity it could not have been started during the holidays', the mistress noted. The foundations were laid on 15 September and during the period that the building work was in progress attendances at the school stayed high. It seems that the children enjoyed watching the work in progress. On 5 December 1893 there were 49 present for a scripture exam.

1893: Congregational Chapel
The Congregational schoolroom in Butt Lane was converted into a chapel in 1893 and opened for worship on 9 February with a service conducted by

Royal Oak and Bemister's Stores photographed in about 1895.

Bere Regis from Poole Hill/Doddings Road in about 1895.

Above: Sheep being driven through the cross at Bere Regis, c.1895.

Right: Horses and carriages about to set off from the crossroads in about 1895 for a carriage competition. Prizes were awarded for dressage and horsemanship and the carriage on the right displays the number '3'.

West Street, Bere Regis, in about 1895. Note thatched barn opposite the stores adjacent to No. 30.

Barrow Hill, Bere Regis, seen from the south west, c.1895. Note the cottage to the north of the Congregational church.

Revd J.C. Smith. The prime benefactor for this, along with the provision of a manse, was grocer and ironmonger Joseph Hamilton Mundell.

1894: Parish Councils Set Up

The magazine circulation had reached 150 copies monthly. On 2 January the new church hall was used as such for the first time. This was the Drax Hall which had been the Congregational Church before the Butt Lane schoolroom-cum-reading-room was converted to that use in 1893, and church Sunday school classes, which had before been held at Butt Lane, were from 1894 onwards transferred to the new hall.

November saw the setting up of parish councils, after which church Vestry meetings would be concerned with purely church matters only. Bere Regis Parish Council was to have 11 members, and the election took place on 17 December, when 161 electors voted out of a possible 230, and 22 candidates stood for the 11 seats.

A jumble sale in aid of a fund to renew sections of the church floor raised the incredible sum of £60.3s.4d. The oak eagle lectern was presented to the church by Mr Radclyffe of Hyde House.

[Information taken from Bere Regis Parish Magazines]

1894: Watercress at Bere

William Bedford established the watercress business at Bere Regis in 1894, having visited the area near Doddings in 1890 from his home in Hertfordshire. He had found ideal conditions for growing watercress with the natural springs and the nearby stream in the river valley. Over the next decade Mr Bedford developed two main beds in the village, that from Doddings, Southbrook called the 'Manor' and another at Roke ('Hollybush'). Further cress production was established at nearby villages.

By 1907 Mr Bedford was in partnership with Mr Arthur Dwight who also ran to Chamberlayne's Farm. He ran the farm and brickworks at Doddings as well. The brickworks ceased operating in about 1912, and by 1920 Mr F. Jesty came into the firm and from that date the name Bedford & Jesty was estab-

lished. By 1924 Bedford & Jesty had become the largest watercress company in the country and were using a trade name for its product: Sylvasprings. Most of the biggest customers were in the Midlands and the north of the country and a sophisticated, rapid, transportation method was developed to ensure delivery of fresh cress all over the country. Another pioneering development was the non-returnable, disposable packaging for the cress, made of thin wood and called 'chips'. The chips contained bunches of cress which were packed at various bed locations.

1894: Most Backward School

The new classroom at Bere Heath School was complete by 6 April but could not be put to use as the wind had blown in a window during early March and not yet been replaced. The new room was used for the first time on 16 May. Summer term ended on 26 July, this also being Miss Horth's last day.

After the holidays Jane Dobson took charge of the school. After she had examined the children she stated that the school was the most backward she had ever encountered.

1895: Mission on Woodbury Hill

As was the usual custom, the caravans of the Itinerant Mission attended Woodbury Hill Fair from Friday 20 to Monday 23 September. As well as providing open-air services, the mission ran a school for the children of fair people, when over 40 attended.

Bere Regis Parish Council formed a committee to consider the possibility of acquiring a Recreation Ground for the village, but it was to be a further ten years before the project could be realised.

During the year 1895 the circulation of the magazine reached 190 copies monthly.

[Information taken from Bere Regis Parish Magazines]

1895: Size of Heath School

The new log book for the Bere Heath School gives the dimensions of the building. The schoolroom was 21 by 16ft, the height to the slope was 13ft and from the slope to the ceiling 4½ feet. The classroom was 18 by 16ft with height to the slope 8½ft. The slope to the ceiling was 1ft 10ins. The length of the school ground from the top of the garden to the end of the boys' playground was 155ft.

1896: Jumble Sale Raises £41
A party of 43 went on a choir outing to Lulworth on Wednesday 15 July by means of 'Mr Day's chara-banc'. Another jumble sale raised almost £41. Such sums (£60 in 1894 and £40 in 1896) were very large indeed at that time.

[Information taken from Bere Regis Parish Magazines]

1896: Poor Roof Repairs
A new roof was put on the schoolroom at Bere Heath School on 29 June but an entry in the log book for 7 October complains that the schoolroom is very damp with water penetrating the new roof worse than before. It claims the water comes through cracks in the walls and floods the floor.

1896: Charles Torreville Leaves School
At the beginning of the year there were 67 on the register at Barrow Hill Boys' School, while on 7 February it is noted in the log book that pupil-teacher John Croft had terminated his engagement and the position of temporary monitor had gone to Tom Marsh. An assistant, Miss Florence Barnes began on 10 April, and on 12 June it is noted that Charles Torreville left school. Two pupils left in September to attend secondary school. In 1897 Charles Tareville [sic] was readmitted for a few days on 30 July whilst on a visit.

1897: Jubilee Celebrations
New gates and piers were provided at the lower churchyard entrance to match those that had already been placed at the north entrance a few years previously.

The diamond jubilee celebrations for Queen Victoria's 'longest reign on record'; consisted of a bonfire on Black Hill, a procession of various village organisations headed by the Puddletown Band, dinner for 360 (cold meat and hot plum pudding), tea for 500, swingboats, a merry-go-round, coconut shies, dancing and fireworks. Altogether £72.3s.11d. was spent on the festivities.

The various winter evening activities included night school, band of hope, choir practice, choral society and woodcarving class. The vicar, the Revd William Farrer was a very enthusiastic wood carver and ran the class referred to, and a bread board made by him sometime after he had left the parish still survives. Its border is elaborately carved with foliage and wheatears, and the inscription reads: 'WB from WF 1913' (to William Bedford from William Farrer).

The harvest festival was held on the usual first Thursday in October, and the custom on these occasions seems to have been for the choir and clergy to process from the vicarage, and to enter the church by the west door.

[Information taken from Bere Regis Parish Magazines]

1897: Congregational Ministers
The ministers of the Congregational church in Butt Lane were as follows: Joseph Blackburn (1897–1906), Lawrence Crookall (1907–1921), J.W. Scamell (1921–1923), J. Gardner (1923–1927), H.J. Wheadon (1928–1936), C.E. Rodhouse (1936–1947), W.L. Duffett (1948–1950), John E. Lauckner (1951–1960), Bernard H. Dawson (1961–1972), Patrick Kellard (1973–1980), Raymond Healy (1980–2001), Jim Morris (2002–present).

1898: 25,000 Troops on Gallows Hill
The parish magazine circulation by this time exceeded 200 copies. Two parishioners had died in 1897, both of whom had reached the age of 97. They were Charles Jesty and William Lugg.

In this year the first group of the Bere Regis Boys' Brigade had been started.

During August some 25,000 troops had been in camp on Bere Heath and on the 24 August a mock battle was

Above: *Royal Oak and the crossroads in about 1896 from one of the earliest series of postcards of Bere Regis.*

Right: *Revd William Farrer, vicar of Bere Regis, tending roses at the vicarage in the summer of 1898.*

staged between Black Hill and Gallows Hill.

During the year a wheeled bier had been acquired to ease the burden of funeral bearers, who, since the establishment of the cemetery in 1881, had been required to walk the whole distance to and from the church.

[Information taken from Bere Regis Parish Magazines]

1898: Discipline Attempt Fails

Barrow Hill Boys' School had about 70 on the register, but on 11 March there was considerable absenteeism due to primrose picking. On 17 June the parents of the worst-offending truants were summoned to the school, but Job Bugby writes in the log book rather dejectedly: 'case dismissed'.

1898: Illness Affects School

The mistress at Bere Heath School, Miss Dobson, is taken ill on 14 February and Harriet Henville became temporary mistress. Miss Dobson returned to her duties on 6 June and later that month attendance is described as being a good average of 42 children. The nationwide diphtheria epidemic of 1898 is not mentioned.

1899: Buddens Lightening Strike

A party of 98 went on a combined Band of Hope and Boys' Brigade outing.

On Sunday 23 July a violent thunderstorm occurred, when over 5ins of rain fell at Wareham, and a cottage at Buddens was struck by lightning.

[Information taken from Bere Regis Parish Magazines]

1899: Death of Headmistress

Miss Dobson, mistress of Bere Heath School was taken ill again on 20 February and Miss Amy Berry from Winterborne Kingston stood in temporarily until 1 July when Anne Elizabeth Cotton took over as headmistress. There were 32 on the register in July, then on 10 August Miss Dobson died of her illness aged 48.

There was a school photo taken by a professional photographer on 25 October and there were 32 children present on that day.

1899: Blackberry Picking

Number on the register at Barrow Hill Boys' School was 72 and on 30 April Ernest Marsh had completed one year as pupil-teacher. Absenteeism was recorded for 15 September due to blackberry picking. Then on 17 November many were absent helping the beaters for a shooting party.

1899: Action in South Africa

Three men from Bere Regis fought in the Boer War in South Africa. They served with the 26th Company, Dorset Imperial Yeomanry's 7th Battalion which was called to arms after the 'black week' of Stormberg, Magersfontein and Colenso, just before Christmas 1899. Colonel Goodden, OC Dorset 'Queen's Own' Yeomanry decided to form a Dorset Company and the Lord Lieutenant, The Earl of Ilchester, called a county meeting at Dorchester. A large sum of money was raised for the purchase of equipment, and the company assembled for the first time at the Royal Artillery Barracks, Dorchester on 6 January 1900. Captain Percy Browne was in command, and the horses had been sourced entirely from Dorset, being bought by Col Goodden and Col Brymer. The Bere Regis men were 5326 F. Shave, 5328 H.H. Tozer and 5330 H.D. Tozer. Embarkation was on 1 March and arrival in Table Bay was on 23 March 1900. First contact with the enemy was on 18 April at the battle of Constantia under General Brabazon's Yeomanry Brigade commanded by Gen. Rundle. The Dorset Yeomanry served in South Africa for over a year. Casualties included four dead, one dangerously wounded, one severely wounded, eight slightly wounded and none missing with no surrenders or convictions by Court Martial. There were three mentions in despatches in the *London Gazette* on 7 May, 10 September and 27 September 1901.

Above: *Church, brewery and pound from Court Green field in about 1899.*

Below: *Dorset Imperial Yeomanry formed up near Dorchester in 1900.*

Chapter 7

The Early-Twentieth Century

Harvest time at Bere Regis c.1900 with Mr Bedford's first binder cutting and binding the wheat in a field south-east of the village. The church tower and the clump of trees on Barrow Hill are on the horizon.

Inset: *Mr Bedford stands next to his binding machine in fields between Doddings and the village c.1900.*

1900: New Vicar for Bere

The Revd William Farrer (who had started the magazine in 1887) left the parish in January, and his successor the Revd W.E.H. Sotheby was inducted on 13 March. The parish clerk, Mr Barnes, had left the parish, and at the Easter Vestry Mr John Battrick was appointed to the post, which he held until his death in December 1957.

In June the choir, which had been hitherto unrobed, were provided with cassocks.

A total of 14 pupils were attending woodcarving classes held on Tuesday evenings during the winter.

[Information taken from Bere Regis Parish Magazines]

1900: Celebration of Mafeking

The Quarterly Summary at Bere Heath School showed that there were 19 boys and 14 girls on the register, but many were absent on 18 April 'gathering primroses to sell'. On 18 May the school celebrated the Relief of Mafeking (on the previous day) by giving the children a longer playtime. The register for 14 November had 21 boys and 16 girls.

Above: *Hayrick building c.1900 on Mr Bedford's farm. Woodbury Hill is visible in the background.*

Below: *Mr Bedford's workforce, photographed at Doddings Farm, c.1900. Left to right, standing: Albert Bedford, Enos Horley, Mr Stickley, Jim Hewitt, Bill Langdown, Fred Hewitt, Jack Joyce, Ernest Day, Frank Hawkins, William Bedford; front row: Harry Hawkins, Henry Davis, Harry Stickley, Charlie Hewitt, Edward Langdown, Charles Cobb, Ted Hawkins, Ian Standfield, W. Standfield, Sam Hewitt, Esan Baker, George Hawkins, Jack Rowland.*

Doddings Farm, Bere Regis, c.1904. There are 23 workers standing in the farmyard and another three people in the garden at the right.

The brickworks at Brick Hill, around 1900. At this time this was run, together with Doddings Farm, by Mr William Bedford.

Above: *The village from Poole Road, c.1900, photographed by Walter Pouncy. A horse-drawn roller is in the foreground and the brewery is visible near the church.*

Left: *Walter Pouncy photograph taken in about 1900 looking toward the church and Westbrook Cottage. Donkey-hauled cart contains 'faggots' (chopped gorse stalks).*

Below: *Chamberlayne's farmhouse built c.1900.*

Doddings Farm in about 1899 with the thatched Flat House (left) and the farmhouse (right), which burned down and was rebuilt in 1904.

1901: London Performers at Concert

The custom of combining the harvest festival service with the thanksgiving for the 1875 restoration of the church was discontinued in this year. From an account concerning the oil-lamps for lighting the village streets, it seems that the lamplighter was paid £4 per year.

Village population from the census was 1014.

At a jumble sale, some entertainment was provided 'and the gramophone, kindly brought by Mr F. Hawkins, gave much amusement.' There was a 'Concert and Dramatic Entertainment' on Friday 27 December, and it was stated that 'The performers are most of them, coming at considerable inconvenience from London, to oblige us.'

[Information taken from Bere Regis Parish Magazines]

1901: Flower Picking Anger

Job Bugby at the Barrow Hill Boys' School notes in the log book his disappointment regarding absenteeism. There were 59 on the register but during the spring term the average attendance was 31. The excuse of 'picking flowers' seemed to have particularly annoyed the headmaster. There was no school on 21 September due to the Fair. The entry for 4 October 1901 states: 'attendance bad. If weather is bad little ones stay away, if weather is good, big boys go out working.'

1902: Tea for 650 for Coronation

It seems that before this time it had not been customary for the congregation to stand at the beginning and end of a service:

I wish to thank the members of the congregation for the ready way in which they have fallen in with the practice suggested from the pulpit of standing when the clergy and choir enter and leave the Church. Some few, I fear, do not quite like the change, but surely its almost universal adoption in other parishes should commend it.

Coronation celebrations for King Edward VII were held on Thursday 14 August, somewhat later than planned, due to the King's lifesaving appendectomy operation by Dorchester surgeon Sir Frederick Treves. There were the usual service, procession, amusements and tea for about 650, and 'as a finale the National Anthem was sung by the choir boys and others on the Church tower, from whence a fine display of Bengal fires lit up the whole village.'

[Information taken from Bere Regis Parish Magazines]

1902: Whooping Cough Epidemic

Problems of absenteeism continue at Barrow Hill Boys' School. On 18 April picking primroses was the main excuse and by the end of the month an average of one quarter of pupils were consistently not present. In early July 1902 there was a whooping cough epidemic and haymaking was another cause of lower attendance, while later in July the excuses were mainly 'hoeing roots'. Then in September a late harvest caused many boys to stay away until the third week, only to be followed by two days' closure due to Woodbury Hill Fair. October saw reduced numbers due to picking potatoes.

1903: Cinematic Film of Coronation

Although perhaps behind the times in the matter of standing at the right time during church services, Bere Regis was at this time very much 'with it' in the field of entertainment, for residents saw what must have been a very early movie film:

On Thursday, January 15th Mr. E. Baker, of Salisbury, gave us a fine exhibition of Cinematograph Pictures of the Coronation, of Seaside Scenes, of a Cricket and Football match, and views of Foreign Countries, diversified with musical performances on a phonograph.

There were 200 children attending Sunday school.

[Information taken from Bere Regis Parish Magazines]

1903: County Council Take Over Schools

Dorset County Council Education Committee took over all schools in the county on 1 June 1903. They also became the managers for the secular instruction in Church Schools of the county. The managers for the Bere Heath School were the Revd W.E.H. Sotheby (vicar), Mr Hibbs, Mr Janes, Mr Marsh, Mr Jesty (representing the County Council), and Mr Bemister (Nonconformist). On 17 June 1903 Mr Hibbs died and there was a big funeral in the village. The schools closed so that all could attend.

Meanwhile, during June and July, there was a lot of absenteeism due to haymaking, then in July monitor Sylvia Gregory's wages of £5 per year is mentioned in the log book. Also in July there were 42 on the register of mixed pupils.

On 13 July 1903 Mrs Hardy's and Mr W. Rawles's cottages caught fire and some of the big boys were sent to give the alarm and get the men in the village to help. However the cottages were totally burnt as well as some of the furniture.

1905: Film Show at Bere

Another 'cinematograph display' was given by Mr Baker of Salisbury to the older Sunday school children on 13 January.

There had been an outbreak of scarlet fever during December 1904, causing two deaths.

The Revd W.E.H. Sotheby left the parish in July, and his successor the Revd Montague Acland Bere arrived in October.

[Information taken from Bere Regis Parish Magazines]

1905: Staff Problems at Heath

A new porch was added to the Bere Heath School at Chamberlayne's in June 1905 and there were 39 on the register. Staff problems seem to have dominated teaching at the school. Miss Cranton had arrived in July 1899, intending to finish on 1 July but was asked to stay on until the end of term on 27 July, which she did. On 27 July Miss Burt began as monitress but was described as being of 'no use'. Mrs Hallam began as mistress on 4 September 1905 and her sister, Miss Webb, began as a supplementary teacher on the recommendation of the vicar, Revd Sotheby. Dorset County Council thought that a monitress at £5 per year would be sufficient. Mrs Hallam's salary of £20 per year was arranged by 28 September, but she left on 31 October 1905. A new mistress, Nellie Marsh, began on 1 November.

Above: *Town's End farmhouse in about 1905. Originally No. 1 and No. 2 Bere Regis, the former was a toll-house until 1871.*

Left: *Revd Montague Acland Bere, vicar of Bere Regis from 1905 to 1919, with his family.*

Below: *Woodbury Hill Fair in about 1905 with Bartlett's Fair 'Galloper Ride' (left) with modifications suggesting a date post-1897. Swing-boats are on the right. Fourth from right is thought to be Tom 'Topsy' Lockyer.*

1905: New Vicar of Bere

Montague Acland Bere was instituted vicar of Bere Regis in 1905. Between March 1916 and April 1919 he served as a chaplain to the forces in France and during his absence the Revd Augustus B. Bennett served as a temporary vicar. The Revd Bere resigned in July 1919.

1905: New Cricket Ground

There was a meeting in the Drax Hall on 25 September 1905 of the cricket club committee where it was decided to acquire three fields behind North Street on the Woodbury Hill side to lay out a dedicated cricket pitch for the village. These fields were farmed by Mr Davis and Mr Kelloway and the cricket committee would be responsible for the rent. This site has been Bere Regis Recreation Ground ever since. The Committee members were Dr Lys, Revd Bere, Captain Palmer, Mr Jesty, Mr Bedford, Mr Dwight, Mr Tozer, Mr Besant, and Mr Bugby. The Revd Montague Bere was appointed captain of the team.

1906: Rifle Club Close Second

In February a visitor's book and collecting box had been placed in the church for the first time, and contributions for the year amounted to £4.1s.3d.

A rifle club had been started, and in its first match against Halifax, Bere Regis were beaten 701 points to 686. The cricket pitch at the Recreation Ground having been completed, the village cricket team was captained during the summer by the vicar, the Revd M.A. Bere, who is said to have been a great cricket enthusiast.

During the summer a number of London children had been on holiday in the village. Bere Regis was one of 18 holiday centres selected by the Victoria Docks Committee, where such holidays were arranged.

North Street c.1906.

[Information taken from Bere Regis Parish Magazines]

1907: No More Afternoon Beer

Some 110 communicants at Easter made the largest number so far recorded.

The Oddfellows and Foresters held their annual fête in the Recreation Ground on Wednesday 19 June, and the vicar had this to say in the magazine:

We hope that the Committee that organises next year's Fete will see its way to stop the sale of alcoholic beverages. We suggest that beer should be provided at the luncheon, but that there should be no drinking tent on the field during the afternoon.

A tennis club had been started with a membership of 35, and a court at Roke Down was used until the two courts at the Recreation Ground were completed.

Bere Heath School photograph of 1906. The headmistress is Mrs Amelia Hallam.

West Street seen from the junction with Butt Lane in about 1910. The police lock-up was the single-storey building on the left. There was no pavement on the south side of the street at this time.

1909: Cricket Successes

During the first week in February a mission was held:

on February 7th, Services were nearly incessant. The Bishop and Mrs. Wordsworth motored over from Lulworth in time for his Lordship to celebrate at 8.30. They stayed with us all day. The Bishop attended six services, preached four times, and confirmed two grownup persons in the afternoon.

The cricket club members had been equipped with green and white caps and ties 'to match the pavilion', and a flag had been given to be flown when home matches were in progress. The team seems to have been very successful at this time, their biggest triumph being on 3 July when they beat the Blandford first XI at Blandford with the highest score the Bere team had so far made 'and created quite a sensation among the cricket enthusiasts in the town.'

Canon Warre who had been vicar of Bere Regis from 1865 to 1876, visited the church and vicarage during the autumn.

[Information taken from Bere Regis Parish Magazines]

1909: Headmistress Resigns

Mrs Hallam, mistress of the Bere Heath School sent in her resignation on 14 July 1909, having been appointed to Shitterton School for Girls. Her last day was 1 October, after which the school closed for a week due to the change of mistress. Mrs M. Satchwill commenced duties as mistress on 11 October. The number on the register was 52 children.

1909: Master and One Assistant

The new log book at Barrow Hill Boys' School commenced on 6 August 1909. The headmaster was Mr Job Bugby, who was helped by one assistant until April 1916. There were 65 boys on the register.

1910: Vicar Hit on Head with Stone

In the March parish magazine a laundry at Culeaze is mentioned.

Referring to the small amounts contributed to church collections, it was stated that at an average Sunday evening service, when the congregation numbered about 200, the collection usually amounted to no more than 5s. or 6s.

The church and the pound, c.1910.

Bere Regis church c.1910.

Above: *Church interior, looking west in about 1910. Oil-lamps provided illumination.*

Right: *Mr Bedford's manor-house seen from Court Green c.1910.*

West Street, Bere Regis, c.1910. On the left is Thomas Applin's butcher's shop while on the right is No. 33 (now gone) and No. 34.

In July the choir outing was to Lulworth, where 'boating was popular, and stone throwing more so. One boy paid off an old score by landing a stone on the Vicar's head.'

Cricket remained popular, there being as many as 200 spectators at a match on 1 August.

The Society of Oddfellows held a Hospital Sunday in October – 'they got together two bands and such a concourse of people as we do not remember to have seen in Church or in the village.'

[Information taken from Bere Regis Parish Magazines]

1911: Tea for 600 for Coronation

The Coronation of King George V was celebrated on 22 June in spite of rain most of the day. The celebrations took the usual form of church service, children's sports, tea for about 600, and dancing, ending with a torchlight procession to Woodbury Hill where a bonfire and firework display were staged. Altogether these events cost £40.14s.2½d., all of which was raised by voluntary subscriptions.

[Information taken from Bere Regis Parish Magazines]

1911: Public Vaccinator Doctor

George Lys, born in Bere Regis in 1867, was the son of Francis Daniel Lys. A physician and surgeon, he married Nora Mary Beatrice Park in 1897 and became District Medical Officer, covering the workhouses in the combined areas of the Wareham and Purbeck Union, the Blandford Union and Wimborne and Cranborne Unions. From 1900, for more than three decades, he was the public vaccinator for each of these areas. The Lys family lived in late-nineteenth-century White Lovington House, on the southern edge of the village, between Southbrook and Rye Hill.

1911: Earning 4s. Per Day

The Bere Heath School register showed that on one day there were 30 present and 13 absent. Five boys were away picking acorns. They received 1s. per

Bere Regis fire-engine was brought into operation after a serious fire in 1911.

96

bushel and could pick four bushels in a day. Miss Hewitt resigned on 21 November and did her last day at the the school on 20 December 1911.

1911: New Chalice

The church plate includes a chalice and lid. The chalice is 6.75ins high and the base is 6.19ins across while the lip is 3.625ins in diameter. The lid is 6.25ins across. There is an inscription on the underside: 'To the Glory of God. In memory of Emily Anne Langford 1876–1886, J.F.L. 1911.'

1911: Census Figures

The population of Bere at the time of the 1911 census totalled 1,059 in the civil parish and 1,442 in the ecclesiastical parish.

1911: Call for a Fire-Engine

There was a fire in Bere Regis which destroyed 'Mr Marsh's premises', probably No. 35 West Street. The vicar in the parish magazine remarked:

... let us hope that some arrangement will be made by which a fire engine can be secured more quickly than is at present possible. In these days it is almost beyond belief that any place should exist so far behind the times, that it relies for the extinction of fire upon water pumped, or even wound up, from a well.

1912: Chipperfield at the Fair

On Lady Day Mr Farr resigned as keeper of the clock and curfew ringer, a post he had held for many years.

He was succeeded by Mr Arthur Janes who continued to do this work until 1956.

The parish magazine circulation was 177 copies per month.

It was in this year that the Bishop first inaugurated the custom of presenting the Easter collections to the vicar, when the amount was £7.18s.9½d., and Bere Regis was the only parish in the Deanery to adopt the suggestion. As Woodbury Hill Fair fell on a Saturday and Monday, open-air services were held on the hill on Sunday, when the choir were mounted on a platform 'outside Mr Chipperfield's booth'.

[Information taken from Bere Regis Parish Magazines]

1912: Headmistress Assaulted

At the Bere Heath School the temporary supply teacher, Miss Atkins, started on 29 January, while on 5 February Miss Randolph started as a supplementary teacher. On 19 July 1912 there were 10 children

Bere Regis from the slopes of Woodbury Hill, c. 1912.

Woodbury Hill Fair in about 1912, probably looking north.

absent out of 45 on the register and the mistress's concerns were noted in the log book that certain families persistently allowed their children to stay away in order to work. She wrote to various officials in an attempt to remedy the situation stating that the consistent absentees were, she considered, backward.

Discipline seems to have been a particular problem at the Heath School at this time. In 1913 only 27 were present from the register of 41 children, this being on 2 May 1913. During an attendance meeting with parents in 1913 one parent struck the headmistress and was subsequently summoned for assault and bound over to keep the peace and made to pay costs of 8s.6d.

1912: Bere Football Club

Bere Regis Football Club was established. The team had joint use of the Recreation Ground, but only off-season when the ground was not needed by the Cricket Club. A team photograph of about 1921 shows the following members of the club: B. Hewitt, F. Brown, R. Ames, A.E. Barnes (trainer), C. Hewitt, G. Griffin, W. Hawkins, B. House, P. Pitfield, W. MacDonald, K. Woolfries and E. Hewitt.

1913: Bere Smock for Queen

At the Easter Vestry, sidesmen were elected for the first time. There were six of them and they made their first appearance as such at a confirmation service on 12 April.

An arts and crafts class was being run by the vicar's wife Mrs M.A. Bere, and several of the members had entered exhibits at the Albert Hall Exhibition in May:

Queen Alexandra bought one of the smocks and a blue pinafore made by Miss Ethel Sheppard. Lord Brownlow, who was conducting Her Majesty round the Exhibition, told her that Mrs M.A. Bere's class

was, he believed, the only class in England at which the real Old English Smocks were reproduced.

The year 1913 saw the introduction of the diocesan quota system, when this parish was required to contribute £12.17s.6d., this sum being raised by a door-to-door collection.

[Information taken from Bere Regis Parish Magazines]

Above: *West Street photographed in about 1912 showing Sheppard's shop.*

Below: *Looking up Butt Lane from West Street c.1912.*

North Street, Bere Regis, looking south in about 1912. No. 104 is on the right while the entrance to the Recreation Ground is on the left.

Chapter 8

War and Peace, 1914–45

The First World War

1914: Church Worth £9,000

Two patrols of boy scouts had been formed with Mr Bertie Jesty as scoutmaster, and they made their first public appearance at a parade and church service on Sunday 11 January.

The following notice appeared in the March parish magazine:

Found. A small piece of wire inside the padlock on one of the almsboxes in the Church, also a hairpin that had been used to try to extract coins from the same. These can be returned to the loser on application at the Vicarage!

In May the church was visited by government surveyors who valued the building at £9,000.

[Information taken from Bere Regis Parish Magazines]

1914: Absences During the War

Attendance at Bere Heath School was a problem all through the First World War. The register was between 37 and 42 during the war and on the worst days typically 40 per cent were absent, on one occasion due to rain. Most of the children had to hike across the fields or tracks to get to school and this was not just an excuse. In the early 1920s the situation recovered somewhat so that on the first day of the autumn term in 1922 there were 99.6 per cent present.

1914–18: Drax Hall Tea Room

The First World War started in August 1914, and although the parish magazine continued as usual, the events at this time are best dealt with collectively for the four year period.

In March 1916 the Revd M.A. Bere departed for France to take up a chaplaincy to the Forces, and during his absence the Revd Augustus B. Bennett acted as a 'locum tenens'. The vicar continued to write a letter for publication in the magazine almost every month during the war, giving details of his work in France, and at the same time keeping in touch with parish affairs.

Major Radclyffe's sturgeon on the roof of his 35 horsepower Daimler in 1914. He had caught the huge fish at Hyde Mill on Bere Heath.

In doing so he passed a newspaper placard proclaiming 'HOTTOBER!' on what must have been the first of October. The Lucas family lived at Mount Pleasant, a cottage beside the Shrubbery on Barrow Hill, where the rainwater butt was empty and the well on the front lawn had failed:

As the drought persisted into the autumn the water came up more and more chalky every day, until at last – nothing! After a hurried consultation it was decided to try and sink the well deeper. A local expert was called in. I remember watching him lower the bucket with a lighted candle in it [to check there was air]. It came up still burning so he decided that it was safe for him to go down. So, with my father and another workman manning the windlass the brave fellow climbed into the bucket and, armed with his pickaxe and shovel, was lowered away. The job took, I believe, two days to complete and countless buckets of chalk were brought up and disposed of, the level being lowered by about six feet. Water, chalky white, began to flow. After two or three days the chalk had settled and the water was drinkable.

Bere Regis from the east pictured c.1920 by E.F. Adams. Court Farm is visible on the left and the manor-house can be seen beyond.

Church interior, c.1920. The pews show up well and the roof-suspended oil-lamps are prominent. The oil-lamps were removed in 1925.

1920: 720 Changes Rung on Bells

It had always been the custom for collections to be taken at church services on the first and third Sundays in the month only, but from March 1920 onwards they were taken at every service.

During the winter season Bere Regis had won the Mid-Dorset Village Football League Cup, having won 10 of their 12 league matches.

The first Parochial Church Council was elected on Friday 16 April and consisted of the vicar, church-wardens and three ruridecanal representatives *ex officio*, and 25 elected members. At its first meeting in June, Miss E. Percy was elected honorary secretary, and held the post continuously until 1952.

On 19 June, 720 changes were rung on the bells by members of the Ancient Society of College Youths. The Revd W. Farrer, a previous vicar who had started the parish magazine in 1887, preached at the harvest services on Sunday 3 October.

The price of the magazine went up from 1d. to 3d. and the circulation was 135 copies per month.

[Information taken from Bere Regis Parish Magazines]

1920: Pupil Goes to Teacher College

At Barrow Hill Boys' School work started on essential repairs on 3 February although the disruption appears to have been minor. The scholars were photographed again on 16 July 1920 and there were 34 on the register. Percy Hewitt passed his pupil-teacher exams in June and left on 23 July to take up a teaching position in Swanage Council School, then on 1 September 1920 Bertie House started as a pupil-teacher. An uncertified supply teacher arrived for work on 8 November to work as an assistant.

1920: Motor Carrier Service

Harry Farr was operating a motor transport carrier from Bere Regis to Wareham on Saturdays and Thursdays.

1920: Outside Bell at Church

The church bells were taken down and sent to the foundry of Mears & Stainbank at Whitechapel, London and completely re-tuned. The tenor bell was made considerably lighter by alterations to the head-stock and canons, etc., and a new treble bell was made. The bells were then returned and placed in a new steel frame that replaced the old timber one. During the time that the bells were away, a temporary bell was slung up on a tree in the churchyard.

1921: Social Club for Ex-Soldiers

The Football Club again won the league cup, having won 12 matches out of 16.

Village population from the census was 970.

The Revd R.C.V. Hodge resigned in October, the new vicar being the Revd P.W. Taylor who was inducted on 19 December. He had been a master at Marlborough College from 1896–1916 and had rowed

Left: *Girls' and Infants' School, Shitterton c.1920, when Mrs Amelia Hallam was headmistress.*

Below: *Barrow Hill Boys' School photo, probably 16 July 1920.*

Bere Regis Boys School

Right: *Hatton's Stores on West Street, c.1920. Mr Hatton is standing in the doorway while Mrs Hatton is at the back door.*

Left: *Shitterton during re-thatching of Nos 3 and 4, c.1920.*

103

Marathon Day was always on 26 December, this picture of spectators being about 1922. Left to right, standing: ?, Mr Mintern, Mr Brown, Jack Miller, Perce Hewitt, Bill Tuck, Mont Cheeseman, Bob Legg, Cecil Hewitt, Charlie Standfield, Ernie Hewitt, ?, ?, Joey Hewitt, ?, Bert Hewitt. Kneeling is Mr Hawkins with children, including Ron Barnes (far right).

1922–25: Women's Institute Hut Opened

In 1923 the Women's Institute bought a hut which was erected on a piece of land at Southbrook forming part of allotment gardens, and which had been given by Mr Ernest Debenham. The hut, another ex-First World War building, was officially opened on 10 July 1923 with a short dedication service followed by a social evening.

In 1924 the social club membership had reached 65.

[Information taken from Bere Regis Parish Magazines]

1923: Mistress Sent Away

At the Bere Heath School Mrs Satchwill was instructed to be transferred to Winterborne Kingston School on 4 January and she left on 28 February. The next day Elsie Martin, a supply teacher took over, but the number on the register had fallen to 19 children.

1924: School Photograph

Pupil of Barrow Hill Boys' School, Robert Lockyer won a scholarship at the end of the summer term. There were 43 on the register and there was another school photograph taken of the boys on 24 October.

1924: New Tennis Club

The Bere Regis Tennis Club was set up. A tennis-court was laid out at the Recreation Ground near the Pavilion but well away from the cricket square. The tennis club paid a half share in a new grass mower which cost £8 in total.

1925: School Numbers Increase

Numbers on the register at Barrow Hill Boys' School had risen to 53 and they had a school photo taken on 2 October 1925.

1926: Dull and Draughty Classroom

At the Barrow Hill Boys' School the pupil-teacher W. Lucas terminated his apprenticeship on 31 March having taken the 'Preliminary Certificate' exam one year in advance and passed with 'Distinction in Arithmetic, Music and Geography'. There was an inspection of the school on 29 March 1926, the report of which noted that there were 51 boys and the head-master taught 33 in five age groups. However, owing to the classroom being 'dull and draughty', the remaining class was taught in the same room by an assistant. A note dated 17 June 1926 suggests that the small classroom was used as a storeroom for gardening tools.

1926: Caps for Cricket Club

The wider use of the cricket ground by other sports resulted in the Cricket Club Committee relinquishing control and a Recreation Ground Committee being set up to run the ground at North Street. During the 1920s the Cricket Club cap was blue with a green motif of a sprig of watercress on the front. The caps were donated by Mr Bedford. By the early 1930s the cap design had changed to green and white stripes.

Barrow Hill Boys' School senior pupils in about 1924–25. Left to right, back row: Gordon Poore, Fred Farr, Edward Ames; middle row: Len Hall, Victor Willment, ?; front row: Ron Barnes, Les Janes, Arthur Mintern, Tom Marsh, Frank Hewitt.

Shitterton School for Girls in about 1924. Left to right, back row: Ada Farr, Rose Hall, Phyllis Stickley, Esther Kellaway, Joan Canes, Phyllis Phillips; third row: Winnie Masterman, Lucy Brown?, Rose Lee Barnes, Beatrice Cheeseman, Winnie Hewitt, Louie Hewitt, Polly Hames, ?, ? Hewitt, Miss Hallam (mistress, 1909–25); second row: Rubbie Stickley, Mabel Legg, Elsie Stickley, Rose Paulley, Nora Barnes, Violet Legg; front row: Florrie Hewitt, Hetti Hewitt, Florrie Stickley, Edie Miller (married name: Edie Green), Mary Applin.

1926–29: Mothers' Union and the WI

In 1927 the Women's Institute membership had reached 55. The tennis club was thriving, with a 1928 membership of 30.

In 1929 two changing-rooms were added at the rear of the WI hut so that it could be more conveniently used for general entertainments.

In 1929 the Mothers' Union membership was 89.

[Information taken from Bere Regis Parish Magazines]

1927: Second Vehicle Bought

George Vacher's Bere Regis Motor Service obtained its second vehicle. A young driver, Reg Toop, had joined the firm some years before, when he was 14 years old. The second vehicle enabled additional routes to Blandford, Bournemouth, Wimborne and Wareham to be added to the Poole and Dorchester runs. The second vehicle was a charabanc which was once pictured with 26 passengers plus the driver.

1927: Post Office in North Street

By 1927 the Post Office had moved from West Street to No. 12 North Street where it remained until 1973 when it was moved back again. The Post Office in North Street was run by Victor Lock and his son, and boasted telephone number Bere Regis 1.

1927: Mr Whiteside, New Master

There were 53 boys on the register at Barrow Hill Boys' School. Miss Yarde was the assistant, while the headmaster, Job Bugby, resigned on 31 December 1927. He had been head since 16 September 1889 and was replaced by Mr H.C. Whiteside on 9 January 1928. Later in 1928 Mr Henry Harvey commenced duties as an assistant, being an 'uncertified teacher', on 3 December 1928. The school finally closed at midday on 30 July 1929 before the summer holidays and Mr Whiteside became headmaster at the Bere Regis Council School at Rye Hill. The building was used for woodwork classes until the craft room at the new school was ready in 1935.

1928: Supply Teacher Runs School

Dorothy Gardiner, headmistress of the Bere Heath School resigned on 30 November 1928 after having worked for six months after recovering from an accident on 30 November 1927 for which she was taken to Dorchester Hospital. There were 26 pupils on the register, and on 3 December 1928 L. Minchinton, a staff supply teacher, took over the school until it closed on 30 July 1929, after which children would attend the Bere Regis Council School at Rye Hill.

1928: Mr Drax Donates Sports Field

The Recreation Ground, which up until 1928 was rented from the Estate, was donated to the Recreation Ground Committee by Mr Drax. The presentation was made during a meeting in the British Legion Hut. Also the ownership of the cricket pavilion passed to the committee, who were responsible for the upkeep of the building and maintaining the grounds.

The Retreat in 1925. It was converted to the present vicarage in 1956.

Woodbury Hill Fair c.1925. In the background (left) is Bartlett's merry-go-round, and at centre a covered circular stall of produce.

Roke Farm in 1927 with Jack Riggs on his tractor.

Above left: *West Street, Bere Regis with Chapman's Stores on the right. Pictured in May 1927, a news hoarding reads 'Lindbergh Crosses Atlantic'.*

Above right: *Bere Regis Motor Service charabanc pictured in August 1927.*

Left: *Butt Lane as photographed in May 1927.*

Barrow Hill Boys' School pupils in 1928. Headmaster Mr Whiteside is top left. Left to right, back row: Raymond Cobb, Frank Hewitt, ?, Arthur Mintern, Fred Farr, Les Jeanes, ?; middle row: ?, Bert Cobb, Jim Farr, Jim Toms, John Hyde, ? Andrews, Tom Marsh, Eddie Ames, ?; front row: ?, ?, ?, Bill Howe, Bob Cobb, Alfie Applin, Len Hall, Jack Hewitt, Vic Willment, ?.

Left: *Bere Regis Motor Service 20-seater at Portsmouth Station in about 1928.*

This picture: *Woodbury Hill Fair in about 1928–29. Bartlett's steam-powered merry-go-round with 'gallopers' turning is in the centre of the picture, with the coconut shy near the front.*

Bere Regis Motor Service charabanc in about 1928 owned by Mr Vacher and driven here by Reg Toop (peaked cap). There are 27 passengers in this picture.

1929: School Opens on Rye Hill

Bere Regis Council School was opened on 16 September, having been postponed from 2 September. The headmaster was Mr Whiteside, and the Rye Hill School took children from across the village.

The schools at Barrow Hill, Shitterton and Bere Heath were closed. The number of children on the register was 150 pupils (91 boys and 59 girls) and there were five staff including the headmaster.

1929: Reg Toop Starts Bus Firm

On 29 October 1929, Reg Toop a driver for George Vacher's Bere Regis Motor Service set up his own company of bus transport based in North Street, Bere Regis. He had financial assistance from a number of Bere Regis people including Dr Lys and Mr Applin, the butcher, to enable him to buy his first bus. His initial routes were Bere Regis to Poole (via Kingston, Zelstone, Lytchett Matravers) once on Mondays and Fridays and four times on Saturdays and Sundays; Bere Regis to Wareham (Thursdays and Saturdays); Bere Regis to Wimborne (Tuesdays); Zelstone via Kingston and Bere to Dorchester (Wednesdays); and Bere Regis to Wareham (via Kingston and Lytchett Matravers) on Thursdays (but only until 1933).

In 1930 Bere Regis & District Motor Service bought two Chevrolets to supplement the Model-T and at the same time acquired the business of James Ironside of Winfrith. Three routes were brought into the business, all from Winfrith; to Wareham (Thursdays), Dorchester (Wednesdays and Saturdays) and to Weymouth (Tuesday and Friday, and from 1930, Saturday evenings).

1929: Modern Cow Milking

Sir Ernest Debenham, as he became with the creation of a baronetcy in 1931, was about to make milking by hand a thing of the past. In 1929 he installed innovative Alfa-Laval milking-machines at eight of his local farms. This was the first such large scale modernisation of dairying in Dorset, which had remained fundamentally unchanged from prehistory through to almost contemporary descriptions in the novels of Thomas Hardy. The formerly intensive labour needs of the rural economy were on an inexorable downward slope.

West Street, Bere Regis, looking west from the Butt Lane junction, c.1929. The steps on the right lead into the First World War hut, while the cottage to the left was struck by lightning and burned down in the early 1930s.

111

Above: *Rye Hill Farm, 1930.*

Left: *West Street and Central Stores in about 1930. Mr Garrett is in the doorway.*

Bedford & Jesty staff photograph at Doddings, August 1932. Left to right, back row: W. Riggs, W. Stickley, F. Wellen, H. James, K. Woolfries, H. Gomer, L. Barter, A. Hookey, G. Hookey, G. Farr, S. Allen, J. O'Reilly, A.G. Goddard, G. Robbins, W. Goddard, W. Hall, D. Hewitt, A. Stanfield, A. Scadden, W. Amey, F. Marsh; seventh row: E.G. Bedford, Mrs Stroud, Miss Selby, Mrs Greening, Mrs Watts, Miss Joyce, Miss Cyphus, A. Courtenay, R. Hardy, R. Ricketts, H.J. Thompson, G. Hames, W. Hall, J. Trowbridge, F. Kent, S. Hewitt, E. J. Presslee, Mrs Read, Miss Hand, Mrs G. Legg, Miss Townsend, Miss Durrant, Miss Smith, H.W. Gregory; sixth row: N. Deakin, Miss Bourne, Miss H, Joyce, Miss R. Pitfield, Miss R. Stickley, Miss D. Stickley, Mrs B. Hewitt, Miss D. Pitfield, Mrs Rawbone, Miss Hall, Mrs Crocker, Miss Day, Mrs Howe, Miss Brooks; Miss Harris. Mrs Bestford, Mrs Fenn, Miss Pittman, Miss Callaway, Mrs Desborough, Miss Goddard, Miss Emery, Miss Hall, J. Nelson; fifth row: F. Lovell, A. Knight, W. Burden, C. Scott, H. Dyke, J. Burden, F.J. Kent, F. Banning, E. Hewitt. C. Hewitt, P. Pitfield, B. Hewitt, W. Priest, J. Chivers, R. Thompson, G. Hunt, A. Brushett, P. Ames, W. Hyde, P. Bartlett; fourth row: C. Mead, J. Goldie, B. Foy, M. Cheeseman, S. Cleall, W. Standfield. R. Joyce, E. Cleall, L. Joyce, C. Standfield, F. Lys, F.T. Jesty, W.P. Stratton, B. Day, J. Lewis, G. Hewitt, G. Cleall, T. Slade, H. Cleall, N. Joyce, R. Sollis, J. Legg; third row: A. Barnes, R. Greening, J. Torevell, L. Standfield, J. Standfield, F. Hewitt, A. J. Goddard, E. Hockey, W. Brushett, Mrs Jesty, W. Bedford, Mrs Bedford, Mrs Stratton, E. Hawkins, F. Townsend, G. Russell, F. Hewitt, J. Joyce, C. Legg, W. Powell, W. Howe, F. Hewitt; second row: W. Hoare, H. Hann, B. Ames, E. Russell, R. Desborough, T. Stroud, E. Hewitt, R. Legg, L. Barnes, J. Legg, L. Rolls, W. Pearce, F. Cleall, H. Pitfield, W. Langdown, W. Hockey, J. Pitfield, D. Leary, A. Bigler, G. Legg, R. Barnes; front row: H. Hewitt, G. Hewitt, E. Bartlett, A. Best, R. Wyatt, A.E. Tuck, F. Farr, W. Toms, H. Hewitt, R. Barnes, F. Cheeseman, A. Legg, A. Lloyd, H. Reed, P. Stickley, E. Rawbone, A. Stickley, W. Tuck, R. Stickley, A. Maidment, E. Ames.

1930: Tennis At Court Green

During 1930 the Tennis Club moved away from the Recreation Ground after Mr Bedford donated a piece of land on the north side of Court Green, near the Cross, for a tennis-court. It was a full-size court surrounded by high wire fences and an iron-frame gate. The tennis-court was only in occasional use by the 1970s, so the land was turned over to allotment gardening.

1930: George Vacher Sells Firm

George Vacher sold his bus business to the expanding Hants & Dorset Motor Company with a condition that he would be employed by them until his retirement. Mr Vacher became the Bere Regis-based inspector working from a small hut and waiting-room on the Dorchester-bound side of the road opposite No. 88, where Central Stores is now located. He died in 1958 aged 71.

1930: Cemetery Lane and Egdon Close

Around this time the first three semi-detached houses along Cemetery Lane were completed on the south side of the lane. The fourth and fifth were added in about 1930. There had been a row of cottages on the south side at the junction with the road at Southbrook but these were demolished in the nineteenth century.

Further along Cemetery Lane, Egdon Close was built in about 1948–52. This development consisted of 11 semi-detached houses and two rows of four houses and aligned with and south of the river.

1930: Kingston Joins Bere

The autumn term began on 2 September at the Bere Regis Council School at Rye Hill. Some 20 senior children from Winterborne Kingston joined the children from Bere Regis.

1930: Chapel Extended

The Chapel in Butt Lane was extended on the north side for a vestry room, storeroom and toilet. The foundation-stone reads: 'Laid by Mr A.W. Backway Treasurer D.C.A. Sept 15th 1930 Minister Revd H.J. Wheadon.' The new length is 70ft (21.5m).

1930s: Bere Versus Oxford

One of the highest profile cricket matches during the 1930s was one organised by Revd Taylor, who was himself an Oxford Boat Race Blue. An Oxford University team visited Bere Regis for an all-day match at the Recreation Ground, ending with much celebration into the evening.

1930–35: Magazine Ceases in 1935

On 17 January 1930 an infant welfare centre was established at the WI hut, held on alternate Friday afternoons, and at the end of its first year of operation there were 45 children on the register.

Village population from the census in 1931 was 1,027.

By 1930 over £860 had been collected by the Bere Regis branch of the British and Foreign Bible Society since its formation in 1847.

The football team had won both the league cup and the Edmonds and Jesty cup in 1930; this double success had only once before been achieved by a team in the league.

In 1930 the village social club was beginning to show signs of a decline, the membership having fallen from 56 to 40.

In 1933 so many children were attending evening handicraft classes at the old Boys' School, that a hut was erected in the grounds to cope with carpentry and engineering classes.

The social club hut in West Street had been closed due to a lack of members, but in 1934 it was reopened for use by the British Legion whose membership was then 138, in addition to 61 in the women's section.

The magazine ceased in 1935 after the death of the Revd P.W. Taylor, who died on 23 October at the age of 74.

[Information taken from Bere Regis Parish Magazines]

1931: Methodist Schoolroom

A schoolroom was added to the east end of the Methodist Chapel. There was a lintel over the doorway with the date '1931' inscribed. An extra 24ft 6ins (7.5m) made the total length 61ft 6ins (18.8m).

1933: Electricity Comes to Bere

An aerial photograph of the centre of Bere Regis was taken at this time. It shows the tennis-court which was set up in 1930 and the recently completed Southbrook Cottages. Behind the church is the Methodist Chapel and the 1931-added schoolroom is obviously a recent addition. There are many barns behind the houses along West Street including the largest – The Old Barn. The key to the date of the photo, however, is the electricity pylons which were installed in 1933. Other points of interest include the immaculate cress beds, the crossroads junction and island with RAC hut, the billiard room on the side of The Retreat (now the vicarage) and the Gentlemen's Club at the Butt Lane/West Street junction.

1933: Lawrence of Arabia

T.E. Lawrence regularly visited Bere Regis on his motorcycle, spending time with locals at the crossroads outside the Corner Shop.

1934: Carved Cross Found

The head of an ancient marble cross was found in a well at Bere Regis, and was presented to Dorset County Museum at Dorchester by Mr Guthrie-Watson.

1935: Barrel Organ Preserved

The early-nineteenth century barrel organ once used in the parish church was donated to the Dorset County Museum in Dorchester by Miss Agnes

113

Above: *Bere Regis & District Motor Services coach in about 1933 outside Briantspuddle School on the Dorchester run. The driver is Tommy Clark.*

Below: *Aerial photograph of Bere Regis taken from the south-east in 1933.*

Charlie Mintern was the 'Hygrade' ice-cream salesman seen here in West Street making a sale to Perce Pitfield and son in June 1933.

Debenham. The description of the organ reads as follows:

The turning of the handle not only revolves the barrel, but also works the bellows. The barrel is a wooden cylinder with metal projections, which as it revolved raised metal catches; these, in turn,

opened valves, which allowed the wind to enter the right pipes. There are ten tunes on the barrel, which is moved slightly sideways to change the tune. Two extra barrels are stored in the cupboard in the organ-stand.

1935: School Hall Begun

Work began on the practical instruction building just north of the school building at Rye Hill. Messrs Boughtons were the contractors for the work, which began on 8 January. It was used for the first time after completion on 2 September 1935, for cookery and woodwork classes. Before this time woodwork classes had been held in the old Boys' School at Barrow Hill. Mains electricity was connected to the Council School at Rye Hill on 9 September 1935.

1935: Tramp Killed

Respectably-dressed tramp William Bywater helped create a carnival atmosphere as Bere Regis celebrated the silver jubilee of King George V on 6 May 1935. He produced a mouth organ in the Drax Arms public house and was accompanied by a local man with a concertina. The atmosphere changed at closing time when a free distribution of beer followed across the street at Kellaway's Garage. Inebriated villagers closed ranks against the tramp and told him to step back. There was some shoving and at least one heavy blow was struck against him. Bywater fumbled in his pocket and produced a razor. A witness from Chamberlayne's on Bere Heath, said Bywater made a dive at the crowd saying, 'I will kill all of you'. He was struck again. Finally, as he staggered weakly away, he was knocked down and given a blow that lifted him off his feet. This caused his head to strike the ground, backwards, resulting in a brain haemorrhage from which he died.

A local man appeared before Wareham magistrates on a charge of manslaughter on 29 June 1935. He was cleared, however, with the case against him being dismissed after a submission that it was justifiable homicide, in defence of himself and the bystanders who were also being threatened by an open razor.

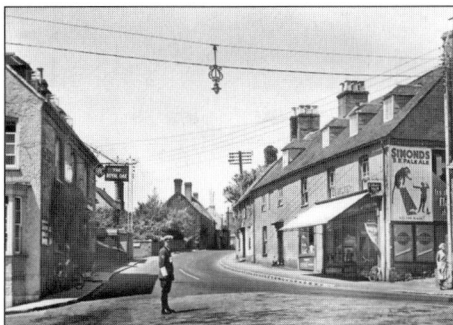

The crossroads in about 1934 with suspended electric lamp above, which was put up in 1933. Bemister's Stores can be seen with its awning.

The crossroads in about 1935.

115

Bere Regis six-a-side football team in 1936–37. Left to right, back row: *Ernie Hewitt, Perce Mintern, 'Squeaker' Sims, John Hyde, Ted 'Dreamy' Bartlett;* seated: *Raymond Ricketts, Cyril Toop, Fred Hunt.*

1938: New Garden at School

At Bere Regis Council School the garden was established to the south of the playground. It would later be turned into a sports field and still be separated by a bank and iron railing with a gate and steps.

1938: Woodbury Hill Fair

There was a Fair on Woodbury Hill in September 1938, but this was the last before the Second World War. It is not certain if the Fair resumed in 1945, but from 1946 until 1951 postwar austerity resulted in an event of declining attendances. In contrast the reliability and popularity of the early fair meant that 'Fair Gypsies' camped on the hill for part of the year. The hiring part of the Fair was much like a slave market, most offering themselves up for work. The strongest were paid the most with the weak glad to get any sort of work. Bere Fair was the loudest, the merriest and the roughest in the West. In the middle ages it had yielded £100 a day to the lord of the manor.

Bere Regis & District Motor Services drivers with coach at the Bere Regis Depot, c.1938. Left to right: *Johnny Bowring, Charlie Ironside, Fred Hann, Bill Ironside, Perce Davis and Arthur Ironside.*

1939: Shitterton Close

The first four semi-detached houses were built in Shitterton Close. The foundations for the remaining two were started in 1939 but work stopped during the war. The fifth and sixth semi-detached houses were completed shortly after the war ended in 1945 and 1946.

1939: Palaeolithic Hand Axe

In about this year a Palaeolithic (pre-3,500BC) hand axe was found by Mr R.E. Burt of Poole on the ground alongside the road from Gallows Hill, Bere Regis, to the crossroads of the Bovington road. The ground had been churned up by tanks which had presumably broken the axe into two main pieces. Both were recovered. The whole axe head is 5.5ins (14cm) long and was made from a large flint flake. One side is greyish and hardly patinated at all, the other side is creamish-white with a small patch of grey and mottled blue, sometimes known as basket-work patina. The find site is about 2.5 miles south of the village centre of Bere Regis.

1939: Death-Watch Beetle

In the spring of 1939 it was found that wood in the church roof was deteriorating. A full survey was conducted by Mr Randoll Blacking FRIBA, whose report stated that death-watch beetle was wreaking havoc, with many of the larger timbers as well as the painted figures being very seriously affected at an alarming rate. The roof needed immediate attention to prevent even more rapid decay, and that a delay of even six months could not be contemplated.

The vicar, the Revd Roland Herring started the Bere Regis Church Roof Restoration Fund with the aim of raising £1,000 to repair the damage. The appeal brochure stated that the destructive work of the beetle was rapidly spreading from the roof to the pews and other woodwork. By the time the contractors erected scaffolding later in 1939, the sum of £800 had been raised to begin treating the roof woodwork with chemicals.

The Second World War

1939: Declaration of War

After the declaration of war against Germany by Neville Chamberlain, on 3 September 1939, one of the first steps taken in Bere Regis, was the excavation of two parallel trenches in the tennis-courts, which together with a small children's area adjoined Court Green to the north. The site was chosen, not it seems for any strategic reason, but because the parish council leased the site. These trenches would have served as protection against aircraft strafing or bomb blast.

1939: Digging of Trenches

Trenches were also dug at the Recreation Ground,

Bere Regis crossroads with Fred Harris on duty in 1939.

again in the children's play area, also leased by the parish council. Digging anywhere near the cricket pitch was absolutely forbidden, but the reaction to the declaration of war meant that First-World-War-type measures were carried out as soon as possible.

1939: Vicarage Billeting

At an early stage of the war, 20 soldiers were billeted at the vicarage during Mr Herring's tenure. This was at what is now The Old Vicarage, previously Summerods in West Street, Bere Regis.

1939: Put That Light Out

Blackout restrictions came into force at an early stage, involving the use of heavy blackout curtains in addition to normal curtains in houses. In public buildings, where such measures were impractical, for example in the church, these buildings could not be used after dark. Vehicles also were subject to blackout rules and headlights were fitted with metal hoods which allowed a small beam of light to be directed downwards. This led to hazardous driving conditions at night. Internal lighting of buses was dimmed down and the windows were covered with a semi-transparent blue film, which gave somewhat limited visibility in daylight. Some people felt nauseous in the dark-blue light inside the buses during the daytime.

1939: Warmwell Activities

The nearby Warmwell airfield also made its presence felt. As well as being a fighter base it was also a training establishment. Almost every day during much of the war a pair of Handley Page Hampdens were droning around with a Fairey Battle trainer practicing attack manoeuvres. In those days aircraft engines required a warm-up period before take-off, and when the wind was in the south or south-west one could hear the roar of a flight of Hurricanes or Spitfires warming up, but they took off into the wind away from the village.

On the other hand, from July 1940 onwards, when the wind was from the north, the warming up could not be heard and there would be a roar as a low-flying group of 12 planes suddenly appeared skimming over Black Hill.

119

The Corner Shop on the crossroads at Bere Regis in about 1940, with Arthur Janes, proprietor.

to D-Day with their tents and vehicles set up in the field adjoining White Lovington.

1940: Troop Transportation
Bere Regis & District Motor Services bought out W.J. Laws's bus business at Briantspuddle in June 1940. He had run services from Briantspuddle via Tolpuddle to Dorchester with one Dennis bus.

1940: Stray Bombs Hit Parish
During the many air raids no bombs fell on the village itself, but there were several nearby. The nearest (and loudest) was on the flat top of Woodbury Hill, which caused some damage to houses there, and further bombs fell in Bere Wood. Another close one was in the roadside verge north of Chamberlaynes, and Turnerspuddle church sustained a direct hit.

There were also clusters of incendiary bombs at Cow Down near Shitterton and in the meadows towards Doddings. Most, if not all, of these local bombs were not deliberate, but jettisoned from enemy aircraft after sustaining damage from RAF fighters, or alternatively the freeing of 'hung-up' bombs and released randomly by the aircraft on their way back to their bases in France. The Heinkel He 111 aircraft which dropped the bombs normally carried eight 250kg bombs in two rows of four in the fuselage.

1940: Tanks Through the Village
The proximity of Bovington meant that tank movements constantly effected the village. Every conceivable type of tank came through the village in convoy from the smaller Bren-gun carriers and British Light Tanks to the larger Valentines, Covenanters, Crusaders and Matildas, and later the American General Lees, Grants, Stuarts and Shermans. The convoys would be continuous during the morning, coming from Bovington, down Rye Hill, past Southbrook, over the crossroads and by way of North Street to presumably Blandford Camp. After a lull over lunchtime, they would all come back again during the afternoon. During one particularly hot and dry period these roads became nothing but a dust track, and the American tanks in particular with their downward-facing exhausts, blew up great clouds of dust as they passed.

1940: Sudden Explosions
Explosives testing was carried out near Clouds Hill and unexpected loud explosions came frequently from that direction, rattling windows and doors in the village. It is believed that the 'Great Panjandrum' (a wheeled rocket-driven weapon) was among many experimental weapons tested there.

1940: Anti-Aircraft Guns
An anti-aircraft battery was stationed at Sleepe, about 5 miles to the east, and their firing was very much in evidence during air raids. A searchlight was set up in the field just to the east of the road between Snatford Bridge and the Wareham road and its powerful beam was a prominent feature during night-time raids.

1940: Invasion Alert
At 2007hrs on the evening of 7 September the order 'Cromwell' was given, to put all Local Defence Volunteers on full invasion alert. Particularly along the South Coast the church bells were rung for the first time in a year. The alert was issued as a result of the first German attack on London and was erroneous, and only meant invasion imminent, not what most thought at the time: invasion by the Germans.

1941: Funds for Spitfires
The Bere Regis Spitfire Fund was set up early in 1941 with a parade around the village with a large model of a Spitfire aircraft on a horse-drawn wagon. In 1940 the price of a Spitfire had been fixed at £5,000, but by later that year was in reality almost twice that figure and continued to rise over the years. Across the country £10m was raised by the public and eventually 900 Spitfires were paid for in this way. This represented a significant fraction of the 18,298 Merlin-engined Spitfires made in total.

Bere Regis Spitfire Fund took off in 1941 with a horse-drawn parade.

1941: Red Bus Brings Evacuees

Evacuees arrived in Bere Regis in a red London Transport double-decker bus, the first time such a vehicle had been seen in the village. The children were taken to their various billets around the village. This sudden increase in the child population had a profound effect on the school, and for a time lessons were held in two sessions, one group attending in the mornings and another in the afternoons. This was later resolved by various reorganisations, including the conversion of the former woodwork room (timber being unobtainable during the war) into a classroom which now forms part of the school hall.

Hurdle-lined trenches dug in fields to the north, adjacent to the school, served as an air-raid shelter during any daylight raids. Children had to carry their gas masks at all times and these were regularly tested by the air-raid wardens who came to the school; all had to don their masks and the warden would ensure that a piece of paper would be retained at the inlet when each child breathed in.

1941: School Numbers Reach 219

At Bere Regis Council School there were 219 children on the register and six staff. The numbers had swelled from 173 in 1940 due to the intake of evacuees to the village. Most had left the village by the next year when numbers had reduced to 179 pupils. Teacher numbers remained the same during the emergency.

1941: Bus Firm Expands

Bere Regis & District Motor Services bought out two transport companies. The first was C.E. Jeanes of Dorchester who operated a Henley via Piddletrentide to Dorchester service that he had started in 1924. he had lately used a Thorneycroft 20-seater. The agreement was sealed in December 1941, the same month that the second buy-out was made. This was the N. Russell firm at Broadmayne. The route was West Knighton via Broadmayne to Dorchester.

1941: Spitfire Forced Landing

Some time in about 1941 a Spitfire fighter made a forced landing in a field just north of Roke Farm on the road to Milborne St Andrew. It may have suffered battle damage but it is more likely that it simply ran out of fuel. Various personnel were called to rescue the aircraft, which only had slight damage to the propeller, including RAF men billeted at Southbrook, Bere Regis. Ten-year-old Fred Pitfield was allowed to go along with the RAF men to see the aircraft. They even allowed him to sit in the pilot's seat. The aircraft's wings were removed and the sections loaded onto a lorry for its journey back to RAF Warmwell.

1941: Secret Churchill Tanks

One June morning three strange tanks unlike anything seen before came through the village, heading towards Bovington. They stopped at the roadside verge opposite the lower church approach so that the crews could stretch their legs and have a smoke. Curious boys were allowed to climb over them and look inside, but were not told anything about them. Next day the three tanks appeared in a press photograph in the *Daily Express*, which stated that they were the first three of a new British tank delivered to 'somewhere in the south of England'. They had, as yet, not been named, but it was likely that they would be called 'Churchills'.

1942: Americans Over Here

In about March, American GIs began arriving in England. Soon after this some were billeted around Bere Regis, while their social and canteen location was at the WI hut at Southbrook.

1942: School Canteen Opens

At Bere Regis Council School at Rye Hill canteen facilities for midday meals began operations on 4 May.

1942: Aerobatic Spitfire

RAF pilots, Harold and Leslie Whiteside, sons of the village school headmaster, on several memorable occasions, flew low over the village, and particularly close to his father's house at the top of Snow Hill.

1942: War transport Needs

Bere Regis & District Motor Service bought out five companies during 1942. War transport enabled a great expansion of the business. H. Hawker of Piddletrentide was taken over early in 1942, a business started in 1902 as a carrier with motor bus services starting in 1916. In February F. Whitty's firm was bought. Whitty had bought the firm in 1938 from Mrs R. Platt who acquired it in 1937 from B. Cox who started it in 1925. Next was F. Thorne of Cerne Abbas with another Dorchester service begun as a carrier by Edward Thorne in 1873, then run by Frank Thorne from 1908. He had used a motor bus since 1913. In June 1942 BR & DM bought E. Markey's company at Winterborne Steepleton who ran a Dorchester service begun in 1932. In September 1942, Ivory Coaches run by L. Sprackling at Winterborne Stickland and Milton Abbas was purchased. There were routes to both Dorchester and Blandford with five vehicles. That firm had started in 1916 with taxi services.

1943: Manoeuvres at Bere

During the latter part of the war various manoeuvres were held from time to time when the village would be thronged with troops and associated vehicles over a concentrated period of several days. The first indication that manoeuvres were afoot was the appearance of working parties laying temporary cables threaded along hedges and under or over gateways alongside the roads. Temporary canvas water tanks, temporary buildings and tents would be set up with groups of vehicles under camouflage netting. These manoeuvres were rehearsals for D-Day, which came in June 1944.

1944: Kitchen Building At School

From 29 March 1944 work began on a dedicated canteen building at Bere Regis Council School adjacent to the playground. The contractors were Marsh of Blandford, but work ceased on 10 May due to a lack of materials during the war. Work recommenced shortly after this and the kitchen was in operation for the first time on 28 August 1944.

1944: More Transport Expansion

Bere Regis & District Motor Services bought out two bus companies in 1944, the first in June 1944 was the G. Lugg company at Hazelbury Bryan. There were two vehicles and routes to Dorchester, Sherborne, Yeovil and Sturminster Newton, all from Hazelbury Bryan. Later in the year BR & DM purchased A. Pitcher's business at Litton Cheney. He had one bus and a route from Swyre via Litton Cheney to Dorchester. Also in 1944, negotiations were begun with G. Churchill of Puncknowle with his Puncknowle to Bridport service in a 1929 Ford 13-seater bus. The deal was completed early in 1945.

1944: Home Guard and ARP Photos

On 15 October photos were taken of Bere Regis ARP (18 members) and the Home Guard (57 members) at the Recreation Ground.

Barn interior at Milborne Stileham, 1943.

1945: New Services to the North

In January 1945 the Bere Regis & District Motor Service bought out the C. Fripp bus company in Okeford Fitzpaine, which ran routes from Okeford to Blandford and Okeford via Manston to Sturminster Newton.

Bere Regis Civil Defence Corps outside the Recreation Ground pavilion on 15 October 1944. Left to right, back row: D. Skinner, L. Barnes, P. Pitfield, M. Miller, middle row: F. Applin, H. Hann, C. Davis, J. Legg, L. Joyce, A. Bartlett, H. Pitfield; front row: K. Woolfries, C. Kellaway, Miss E. Lys, J. Strang, Miss G. Miller, W.F. Lys, E. Hewitt.

Chapter 9

Modern Bere and the New Millennium

Postwar Recovery

1946: New Vehicles for Bus Firm

Bere Regis and District Motor Service bought ten new Bedford buses together with some second-hand buses, which included two Leyland Titan TD4s, the firm's first double-decker buses. The bigger seating capacity vehicles were normally used on the Bere Regis to Poole, Bere Regis to Dorchester and Dorchester to Sherborne routes. A further Leyland Titan was purchased in 1948. Two more modern (1947 vintage) Leyland PDIs were added to the fleet in 1949, which were ex-Hants & Sussex buses and were in use until 1960.

1947: Severe Winter

During January and February there was a most severe cold spell with snow lying for several weeks and repeated snow falls after attempts to clear it away. The conditions affected building work in the village, travelling to work or school, and in particular Bere Regis & District Motor Services had huge problems keeping buses going and meeting their timetabled service responsibilities. To add to the difficulties, postwar austerity lead to food shortages and power cuts.

1947: Green Close

Eight semi-detached houses were built south of the school on Rye Hill from about 1947 to 1948. The development was called Green Close, after the name of the field to the north of the school. The field on which they were built had been used as a sports area by the school after haymaking and in the off-season months, and even had a trench dug as an emergency shelter for the children at the school during the Second World War. The sports field, as it is now, was a school garden until 1953. In the late 1980s or early 1990s three more buildings were added to the east end of Green Close including houses and semi-detached buildings.

1947: Hardy Fans and Ringers

The pattern of visitor flows were inevitably interrupted by the Second World War but by July 1947 Bere's vicar, Revd R.C. Herring, was writing that arrivals had resumed and had reached 700 a week.

One particular trip that was long remembered comprised nine bell-ringers from Loders, in a coach from Bridport, who stepped out into a gale with 20 supporters and their self-styled 'brewer and chaplain' in 1948. He was a new vicar from those parts, Revd Oliver Willmott, whose passion was IPA – India Pale Ale – which he brewed and bottled in Loders vicarage. The group had stopped off during a journey to Portsmouth in order to ring Bere bells. They also seem to have reached the Drax or the Oak as the vicar recorded in the parish magazine that they 'proved alarmingly expert at pulling of another kind'.

1948: Huge Depot Shed

Around this time the Bere Regis & District Motor Service built their huge depot garage at the bottom of a driveway opposite the Drax Arms public house and next to the Methodist chapel. Previously some cobb-walled outbuildings and barns were used. There was a yard for turning and parking buses between the garage and the chapel. By volume it was the largest building in the village and was 120ft long and 60ft wide going east–west and having a

Mr F. Shave farming traditionally at Rye Hill in the 1940s.

Bedford & Jesty Sylvasprings lorry at Doddings, c.1948.

Above: *Egdon Close, Bere Regis was built between about 1949 and 1952.*

Right: *Bere Regis & District Bedford OB/Duple 29-seater bus at the Bere Regis Depot and behind the Methodist chapel. BR & DMS had bought two of this type of vehicle from Hants & Sussex in 1949.*

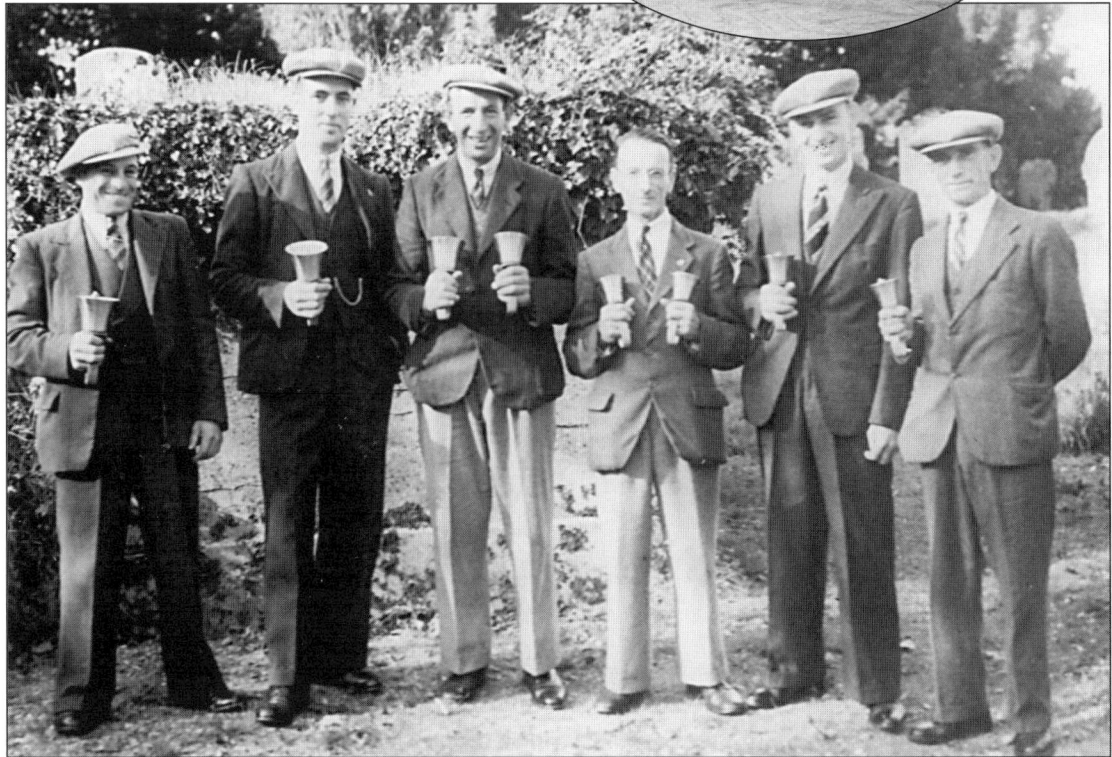

Bere Regis ringers with hand bells in about 1949. Left to right: Arthur 'Matt' Stickley, John Cleall, Giles Cheeseman, Ed Rawbone, Raymond Ricketts, Harry Pitfield.

double-pitched roof. Construction was mainly of iron girders with corrugated-iron and asbestos sheeting. Before this time the buses were parked along the hedge of the field that reached down to the river.

The garage was finally demolished in the 1980s during development of housing and Turberville Court. The only remains are some of the retaining wall which now forms part of the entrance driveway for Turberville Court, while part of the present car park is an indication of its previous position.

1949: Roman Road

In July the Royal Commission on Historical Monuments excavated part of the Roman Road at Bagwood Coppice. This established the existence and position of the extensive settlement remains.

1949: Cricket Committee

With the return to sporting activities after the war, a new cricket committee was set up at the Recreation Ground. A new pavilion was built to replace the old one with the luxuries of both water and electricity being laid on. Both these utilities were essential to providing teas at cricket matches.

1950: Grammar School Selection

Children from Bere Regis Council School sat grammar school entrance exams at Poole on 17 March 1950. The headmaster, Mr Whiteside, attended a selection panel at Poole Grammar School on 19 June 1950, but with the imminent introduction of the 11+ exam, this was the last time that successful entrants transferred to the grammar school.

Early in the autumn term the school was closed on 21 September so that the children could attend Woodbury Hill Fair as usual.

1950s: Tennis and Cricket

The Tennis Club put a new court in at the Recreation Ground and remained there until the court at Court Green was repaired after war use. Those repairs included some of the area being tarmacked.

The Cricket Club recruited many good players from the village, such that the team became one of the strongest village sides in Dorset. During the 1950s the Bere Regis team won the Dorset Evening League six times and the Knockout Cup several times. They even beat Dorchester Wanderers in a particularly low-scoring match by 29 to 28 runs, Dorchester being 18 for 8 at one stage! Matches were also played against Weymouth, Blandford, Poole Park, Bournemouth 2nd XI, Broadstone, Portland, Bournemouth Gas Works, Milton Abbas, Bryanston School and Bournemouth Water Co. Transportation to these fixtures was often provided by Bere Regis & District Motor Services coaches. Bere Regis cricket thrived for many years, but by the late 1960s the number of enthusiasts declined and matches ceased in 1970–71.

Townsend farmhouse pictured in about 1950.

Bere Regis Football Team, c.1950–51 at an away venue. Left to right, back row: Charlie Lockyer, George Henson?, Jonnie Barnes, ? Stickland, ? Bennett, Alan Davis; front row: Jimmy 'Curly' Cobb, Raymond Ricketts, Charlie Crocker, ?, Randolf 'Randy' Barnes.

West Street, Bere Regis, looking west in about 1951 from a postcard series. On the right is the brick-fronted Nos 55, 56 and 57, while on the left No. 40 is offering teas.

West Street, Bere Regis, in the early 1950s. The hut on the left was Mr Vacher's waiting-room and office as bus inspector for Hants & Dorset until about 1952.

Bere Regis Fire Station was built by Messrs Griffin in 1951 in North Street. This picture was taken in May 1991 during refurbishment work.

Corner Shop with Arthur Janes sitting outside, c.1952.

1951: Romano-Belgic Pottery

In January some Belgic or Romano-British pottery was found during the digging of a trench for a pipe at Muddox Barrow Coppice, Bere Regis. It was noticed in a spoil heap by Miss Lyster, a Land Girl working for Mr John Strang of Bere Down Farm. The trench being dug was 2ft wide and a mechanical excavator was being used near the north corner of the field north-east of Muddox Barrow Coppice, grid reference SY8539 9689. The trench was about 2ft deep and the pieces were found at the deeper level. The finds were examined by Lt-Col C.D. Drew who recovered several pieces of coarse ware including a poorly turned semi-solid pedestal base of coarsely gritted black ware unevenly fired to reddish in places.

Above: *Cattle being driven through West Street, Bere Regis, c.1953, from Manor Farm to fields near Butt Lane.*

Below: *Cress picking at Southbrook c.1955.*

Top: *Bere Regis School hockey team, late 1930s. Left to right, back row: Elsie Stickley, Violet Stickley, ?, Diane Ames; middle row: Nora Barnes, ? Snarchell, ? Lloyd; front row: Peggy Janes, Mary Battrick, Eileen Barnes, Margery Applin.*

Above left: *The Old Barn service station in November 1988 when it was for sale.*

Above right: *White Lovington Cottage, Southbrook, in about 1955 and now gone.*

Left: *Bemister's shop girls in about 1955. Left to right: Jean Gerrard, Cythya Cleall, Valerie Cheeseman, Angela McDonald. The photo was taken by Irene Hunkle and the little dog is called Sadie.*

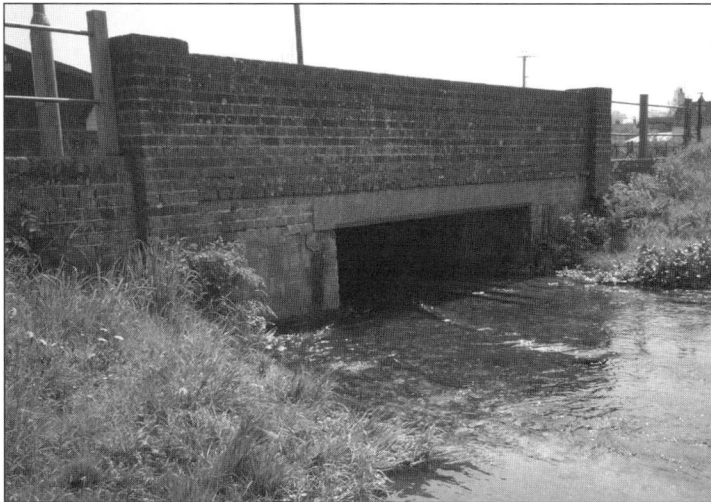

Top left: *The Old Barn, West Street in 1956 shortly before demolition to make way for the Esso service station.*

Top right: *The Retreat, now the vicarage during renovation in 1956.*

Left: *Southbrook Bridge pictured in 2006.*

Below: *WI hut event of about 1956.* Left to right, back row: *Edith Hewitt, Beat Cleall, Pauline Jesty, Mrs Griffin, Mrs Brown, Mrs Osmond. Two men at the back are helpers;* front row: *Mrs Percy, Mrs Janes, Mrs Bedford, Mrs Anderson, Mrs Henson, Mrs Bowditch, Mrs Applin, ?.*

1951: Census Figures

The population of Bere Regis from the census of 1951 totalled 1,130.

1952: New Cloakrooms

In December work began on a new cloakroom and lavatory block on the east front of the building at the Bere Regis Council School on Rye Hill. The contractors were Messrs Griffin. The number of pupils on the register was 190 and there were seven staff.

1953: Primary School

The new cloakroom and toilet block at the Bere Regis Council School was attached to the main building. It had a flat roof and was completed in October 1953. From then the toilets at the bottom of the playground ceased to be used. At the same time the existing smaller cloakrooms at each end of the school building were converted to a staff room at the north end and a boiler room at the south end. Numbers on the register were 107 and there were four staff.

Autumn term began at Rye Hill on 7 September as a Primary School, only taking children up to the age of 11. Staff numbers reduced from seven to four. Children over the age of 11 proceed to Bovington Secondary Modern School, except those passing the 11+ exam who transferred to Blandford Grammar School.

On 15 December the school garden was levelled to form the playing-field. It was big enough to play cricket and football, although the slope always favoured spinners bowling from the meadow end. Also in December 1953 the partition wall between the two practical instruction rooms was removed to form the school hall.

1954: Ex-London Buses

Bere Regis & District Motor Services acquired three ex-London buses to add to the existing fleet of the expanding company.

1955: New vicarage

The vicarage, later called Summerods was sold to be used as a private house and The Retreat was bought for the new vicarage. It was altered and improved, in particular by the demolition of the billiard room on the south side. The vicar, the Revd Herring moved in to the vicarage in June 1956.

1956: Cold War Comes to Bere

The road at Southbrook was widened in 1956 following the removal of its brick-built eighteenth-century bridge which was replaced by a single slab of reinforced concrete. The nearby Women's Institute Hall, in an ex-Army wooden hut dating from the First World War, was also due for demolition, but instead survived until 1987. An underground concrete bunker, built inside the prehistoric rampart on Woodbury Hill, was used as a Cold War radiation monitoring post of the Royal Observer Corps.

1956: Black Hill Reservoir

Water mains came to the village during 1956 with West Street being switched on first, in July. A reservoir had been built on Black Hill on the south-east side to provide pressure for the system.

1956: Old Barn Service Station

The Old Barn Service Station was built and formally opened in 1956. It was situated on West Street Bere Regis, between No. 36/37 and No. 38 on the site of the former 'old barn'. An official ribbon-cutting ceremony was performed by Mr W.R. Lewis, district manager, Esso Petroleum Co. Ltd, Exeter. The enterprise had been set up by Mr and Mrs Jarvis.

1956: Ready-Cooked Steaks

At about 12 noon on 20 December 1956 the butcher's van of Messrs Applin & Sons caught fire in West Street, near the butcher's shop. The fire brigade arrived and eventually put it out, although the van was completely burnt out. Messrs Frank and Maurice Applin who were on the scene showed concern, but onlookers who had gathered seemed to be more amused than otherwise, and jests referring to 'ready-cooked steaks' could be heard.

1957: New Headmaster, Mr Endacott

On 27 May during road widening, the Sarsen Stone on the verge near Court Green was moved up to Bere Regis Primary School near the south-west entrance gate.

The last day of term at the school was the last working day for headmaster Mr H.C. Whiteside, on 31 July 1957. His resignation was to take effect from 31 August. The school reopened on 11 September with Mr S.J. Endacott as the new headmaster.

1957: Any Questions at Drax Hall

The Drax Hall was declared open on 4 October, by Lt-Cmdr H.W. Drax, R.N., followed by the broadcast of the BBC Light programme 'Any Questions' from the Hall, hosted by question-master Freddy Grisewood. The celebrity panel comprised Mary Stocks, Sir Stuart Wilson, Tom Driberg and John Connell.

The opening ceremony on 4 October followed extensive work to add an intermediate floor and stairwell, and at the ceremony was given to the village, it having been leased from the estate before then. The repairs had been paid for by raising about £2,000 over the years, while the Ministry of Education had given a grant of £1,090 and the National Council for Social Service loaned the project £1,600 subject to guarantors coming forward. The chairman of the Building Hall Committee was Mr John Strang, who presided over the official opening,

The 1960s and 1970s

1960: Bloxworth Children
Bere Regis Primary School autumn term began on 14 September and included children from Bloxworth following the closure of Bloxworth School earlier that year.

1960: Fire Brings Play Area
Two cottages were lost to fire in 1960 at Tower Hill, Bere Regis. The joined cottages were both originally No. 70 and occupied a position opposite the Tower House entrance on the lane joining Butt Lane to Barrow Hill. The remains of the cottages were not cleared away for some time and became a play area for local children until the late 1960s. A new house was built on the site in the 1990s.

1961: Biggest Independent Bus Firm
By this year the fleet of the Bere Regis & District Motor Services had reached 92 vehicles. The makes of vehicle included AEC, Bedford, Commer, Daimler, Dennis, Maudsley and Leyland. The Leylands were Tigers, Tiger Cubs and Royal Tigers, while all but one were coaches. There was one bus, a Daimler Freeline model, and included were five minibuses of several types but all 11-seaters. Many of the vehicles were second-hand, but the fleet included 12 Bedford coaches that were bought new in 1959 and 1960.

1961: Open Prison Founder Dies
On 23 November 1961, Mr William Wigan Llewellin, OBE, died at White Lovington, Bere Regis, aged 72. Educated at Eton and University College, Oxford, he served with the Dorsetshire Regiment during the First World War, becoming Captain in 1917. In 1922 Mr Llewellin was appointed headmaster of Portland Borstal Institute and worked unstintingly in Borstals until he retired in 1949, when he received his OBE. During that time he had founded the idea of 'open' prisons in England and Wales.

He was appointed a JP in 1950 and was a member of the Wareham Bench from 1951. Mr Llewellin was the High Sheriff of Dorset in 1956. Since moving to Bere Regis on retirement he had been active with the British Legion and other charities, and was a lay reader at the parish church.

1961: New Vicar for Bere
Revd Paul Trevor William Tranter was instituted vicar of Bere Regis on 16 February 1961. At the end of his time here, a farewell presentation was made by the churchwardens and the PCC on Friday 29 October 1976 at the Drax Hall. Mr and Mrs Tranter retired on Sunday 31 October 1976 and moved to Child Okeford.

1961: Population Census
Village population from the census is 1,157.

1962: Sewerage System Decision
Wareham and Purbeck Health Committee decided by majority vote that Bere Regis would get priority for a main sewerage system over the parishes of Studland

Carnival float, June 1961. The WI's 'First Outing' and first-prize winner. Left to right, standing: *Elizabeth Wyatt, Peggy Wyatt, Beat Cleall, Mrs Osmond*; seated: *Phyl Hopkins, Jane Wyatt, Sally Cheeseman, Mrs Andrews.*

and Lytchett Matravers. The work was eventually carried out during the next two years, mainly by the firm Tillbury Maidment, manned in no small way by Irish labourers.

1962: Siren Too Loud for Some Residents

At the fire station in North Street, a tower-mounted siren was fitted in April 1962. Representations from the Bere Regis Parish Council advised that a baffle be fitted to the siren itself, in order to reduce the noise for those living close to the station. The sound of the siren in the village was familiar to residents through the 1960s and into the 1970s when radio pagers replaced the calling system for the at-readiness firemen of the village.

On 30 December 1962 Bere Regis found itself cut off by snow. West Street looking east with the Esso filling station on the right.

1962: Falling Numbers Close Chapel

The Methodist chapel at Bere Regis was closed due to lack of support. The chapel, at the end of a small lane opposite the Drax Arms and alongside the Bere Regis & District Motor Services garages, was built in 1890 and closed early in May 1962. It had been known for some months that closure was likely, and the building was later sold to the building firm, G. & L. Barnes for a carpentry workshop.

1962: Gliding Club Established

In May the Blackmore Vale Gliding Club applied for planning permission to use land at Gallows Hill, Bere Regis for a gliding site. The application was eventually approved and since then the site has been very active with, at first, aircraft-towing glider flights and, later, the use of a winching system.

1962: Church Garden Party

The parish church garden party held on Saturday 30

Aerial view above Bere Down in 1962 showing extensive ancient field markings.

June 1962 raised £152 toward the envisaged £700 needed for essential rewiring repairs to the church. The garden party was held in the garden of Brigadier and Mrs Tadman, Summerods, West Street. It was opened by Lady Debenham, with the Revd Paul Tranter officiating. National and maypole dancing routines were performed by the children from the school under the direction of headmaster Mr S.J. Endacott. The stalls included: Mothers' Union, cakes, groceries, new things, white elephant, produce, orangery, tombola, teas, competitions, flowers, mile of pennies, roll-a-ball, roll-a-penny, balls in drainpipe, dog race, treasure hunt and table skittles. Other fund-raising events included a flower festival in the church, which raised £370. The dedication service for the repairs followed on 23 June 1963, by the previous vicar, the Revd R.C. Herring.

1962: Manor Sells Cottages

An auction by Fox & Sons of Bournemouth, organised by Lt-Cmdr Plunkett Ernle-Erle-Drax, RN, on Thursday 26 July resulted in the sale of two Bere Regis cottages. No. 34 West Street was sold for £2,025, while No. 14 North Street changed hands, freehold, for £850.

1962: Driver Bruises Knee

On 19 August 1962 there was an accident on the road toward Dorchester. A lorry belonging to Habin (Haulage) Ltd of Southampton was loaded with hundreds of cases of tomatoes and it is thought that a shifting load caused the vehicle to leave the road, plough through a hedge and finally come to rest leaning against a telegraph pole. The boxes of tomatoes fell into the field adjacent to the road to Milborne St Andrew. The driver, who for obvious reasons, refused to give his name, suffered a bruised knee. The next spring a large number of tomato plants were growing near the spot.

1962: Bagwood Coppice Digs

The Romano-British settlement at Bagwood Coppice north of the village on Bere Down was investigated during three weeks of August 1962 and a similar period in 1963. Lead investigator of the digs was Mr Geoffrey S. Toms, classics master at Birkinhead School and son-in-law of Mr Charles Cape, the former assistant of Mr William Llewellin at the Borstal Institution. The team of diggers consisted of a dozen archaeology students from Oxford University and eight boys from Portland Borstal, the latter being rotated each week. The whole team

135

camped on Bere Down in tents and three or four WVS volunteers provided meals each day.

In 1962 Mr Toms had made a 4ft (1.2m) wide trench across the 5 acre (2 hectare) area of interest, and found remains from the second century AD. Aerial photographs were taken of the area during the following winter so that the 1963 dig could target specific markings on the ground. The oldest find was a Roman coin of the Emperor Trajan (98–117AD) and overall revealed a farming unit that had been occupied from about 120–360AD. It is thought these people lived in huts of clay, wattle and daub, used Roman coinage, pottery and possessed brooches, bronze finger rings and used weaving machines. Some of the pottery was Samian while other coins bore the heads of Trajan's sister Marciana, and the Empress Faustina.

The use of Borstal boys along with Oxford boys was part of the legacy left by Bere Regis resident William Llewellin (1889–1961) and bore fruit with at least one young Portland Borstal offender. When he returned home to Sussex he became an enthusiastic member of his local archaeological society in late 1962.

1962: Temporary School Head

Mr J.R. Litson took over as headmaster at Bere Regis Primary School from the autumn term in September, while Mr S.J. Endacott went on a year's sabbatical working as a lecturer at Weymouth Teacher Training College. Mr Endacott returned to his position of headmaster in September 1963.

1962: Harvest Supper

On Saturday 6 October 1962 the village Harvest Supper was held in the Women's Institute Hall, Southbrook. This started a village tradition that would last out the Revd Paul Tranter's tenure as vicar, until 1978, when the Revd Dennis Shaw was the vicar. Over 100 parishioners and friends were present at this 1962 Harvest Supper, welcomed by the vicar, the congregational pastor and Mrs Dawson, the pastor's wife. After the supper there were talks, musical pieces, including part of a brass group, songs with piano and recitations and readings in Dorset dialect by Mrs Lewis of Bere Heath.

1962: Ploughing Match

The Wareham & Purbeck Young Farmers' Club put on a ploughing match on Bere Down Farm on 19 October 1962. This annual event had been held at various places before, but on this occasion was hosted by Mr Ireland. There were 22 entries.

Quintuplet sheep birth at Bere Regis in 1963.

1962: Divided Loyalties

At the centre of the hustings on 19 November 1962, Bere Regis hosted both main prospective members of Parliament for the by-election of 22 November. The South Dorset constituency had been long regarded as a safe Tory seat and Mr Angus Maude was confident. However, Sir Piers Debenham was running on an Anti-Common Market ticket, which on the Thursday had split the conservative vote, such that the Labour candidate, Mr G. Barnett won the seat.

1962: Music in Butt Lane

The Congregational chapel in Butt Lane had a new electronic organ installed. The money had been raised by subscription and by various fund-raising events such as jumble sales and concerts. It was first used publicly on 20 December 1962 when the Swanage Congregation Church Women's Choir visited. The collection raised £6.14s.6d.

1963: New Butcher at No. 85

With the death in February 1963 of Mr Gilbert (John) Applin, aged 62 years, the butcher's shop at No. 85 West Street ended the Applin butchers' name that had begun in 1885. The business at No. 85 West Street was taken over by Charles Jeeves who continued until retirement in the 1980s. From then the shop became a Spar mini-market.

1963: Quintuplet Lamb Birth

In March quintuplet lambs were born on the farm of

The Women's Institute carnival float c.1963 had the theme of pub names. Standing, left to right: *Mrs Crocker, Mrs Percy, Mrs Cleall, Mrs Osmond, Mrs Wyatt;* seated: *Joan Cleall, Mrs Andrews.*

Mr Thomas Snow at Roke Farm, Bere Regis. They were born to a black-faced sheep who was feeding two, while villagers were looking after the other three lambs. A Ministry of Agriculture spokesman said that the chance of lamb quintuplets was more than a million to one.

1963: Trying to Save Barrows
The Ministry of Works statutory scheduling for the preservation of dozens of ancient monuments in Dorset was announced on 16 May 1963. They include three round barrows north-west of Millum Head, Bere Regis and a round barrow on Gallows Hill, Bere Regis.

1963: Prince and Princess at Carnival
Bere Regis Carnival was opened on 8 June by Prince Carol and Princess Jeanne of Romania. The parade was led by the British Legion Branch carrying 20 fluttering standards, followed by the Durnovaria Silver Band from Dorchester. Once at the Recreation Ground there was a parade of hounds by permission of the South Dorset Hunt, while Dorset Police put on a show with their dogs. There was a comedy act by The Brooklyn Trio, then country dancing by pupils from the school. There were static displays by the Dorset Regiment, the Territorial Army and the Boy Scouts.

Total attendance at the carnival was estimated at 3,000 but the high spot of the day was the evening procession which included a fancy-dress parade. The day ended with dancing in the Drax Hall. Despite the success of the carnival, the final accounts showed a loss of £10 for the day, the first loss in its eight-year history.

1963: Traffic Lights Cause Tailback
Bere Regis Parish Council, supported by Dorset County Council, in October, petition the Ministry of Transport for the installation of traffic lights to be set up at the crossroads where the A31 meets the A35.

Also in October, street-name boards were given approval, although only three would be provided at a cost of £12. The other seven streets or roads would have to wait a little longer to be signposted.

Traffic lights at the crossroads in Bere Regis were in operation for the first time on 24 August 1964. On the first Saturday that the lights were in use, on 29 August 1964, the bank holiday weekend, a queue of vehicles stretched as far as the top of Dorchester Hill on the west side of the village. The street lighting fittings were renewed on 15 September 1964, and several new lights were installed around the village. Street-name boards were put up around the village in October 1964.

1964: Bere Regis From the Air
An aerial colour photograph was taken of the village in about 1964. The photo was taken from the south-east and at a height of about 2,500ft (760m). At this

Aerial photograph of Bere Regis taken c.1964 from the south-east.

time Boswell's Close had not been started, the area being a field. South Mead, which started in 1966, is occupied in the picture by the Bradford's Coal Merchants yard and buildings. The biggest building

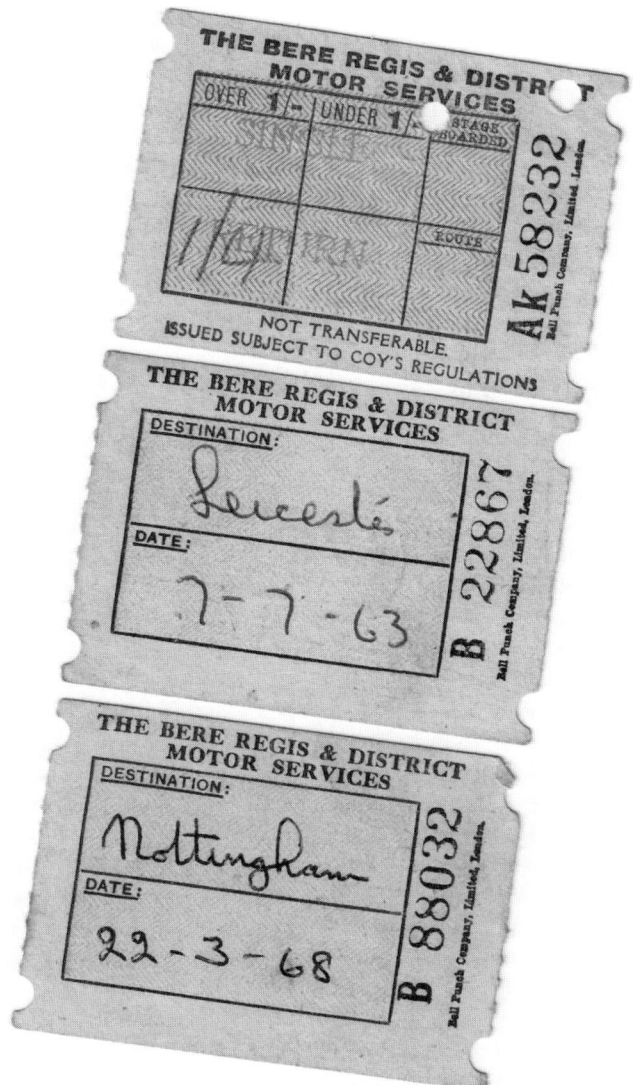

Bere Regis & District Motor Services 1960s bus tickets.

General view of a fête at Bere Regis in the garden of Summerods in June 1964.

In June 1964 the carnival was formally opened by Miss World Anne Sidney, seen here with Bere resident Arthur Janes.

after the church, but covering a larger ground area, is the Bere Regis & District Motor Services shed to the west of the church and the meadow to the river goes right up to the back of the houses on the south side of West Street. White Lovington House is visible, as are the barns and houses at the point where Rye Hill begins to rise from the river valley. The village is surrounded by many more fields with a lot of hedges still in place before removal.

1965: Boswell's Close
A housing development of 16 bungalows was built on Snow Hill where it curves towards Chalkey Lane. The land slopes down toward North Street and when completed in 1966 is called Boswell's Close. It was named to honour J.W. Boswell (and his family) who was the first professional photographer of Bere Regis from 1863.

1965: New Headmaster
On 28 April 1965 Mr E. Alan Stacey took up duties as headmaster at Bere Regis Primary School, taking over from Mr H.S. Williams who had deputised in the position since Mr Endacott's resignation on 31

December 1964. The Parent Teacher Association (PTA) was founded on 28 September 1965.

1965: Queen's Sister Passes Through
Princess Margaret passed through Bere Regis on 25 June, on her way to Puddletown, via North and West Streets. She was opening the new secondary modern school at Puddletown.

1965: The Winston Factor
The world's biggest dog, Winston died at his owner's home of No. 8 Shitterton, Bere Regis in August, aged nine years. The dog's registered name was 'Sir Winston' and owner Miss Ivy Love, revealed that he ate 20lb (9kg) of meat a week, mixed with vegetables, and drank a pint of milk a day. The St Bernard weighed 17 stone (108kg) and was 6ft 2ins long and 3ft 2ins high at the shoulder.

Miss Love attributed the dog's great size to the amount of food that he ate as a puppy, while the cost of feeding Winston was assisted by a legacy from Mr Claxton of Martinstown. He was one of a litter of ten puppies, unusual for the breed as a St Bernard bitch normally only produces one or two puppies. Miss Love said that Winston was a good guard dog, but was friendly and even allowed kiddies to ride on his back. He did not bite, but he had been known to pin a stranger to the wall. After Winston died, Miss Love got another St Bernard, which she called Winston II later in September 1965.

'The biggest dog in the world' Winston with owner Miss Love in December 1963.

1966: South Mead

A housing close of 16 bungalows was built in Bere Regis and called South Mead. It is between No. 39 and No. 40 West Street with the land falling slightly toward the river valley and was formerly the field attached to No. 40. There had been a large barn set back from the road but this was almost totally destroyed by the whirlwind of 1959. A brick wall had run from a gate next to No 40. to No. 39 and the Bradford's coalyard. Bungalow completions were from 1967.

1967: Single-Colour Rainbow

Work began on the main sewer for Bere Regis by the contractors Tillbury Maidment Ltd. Up until this time most of the newer houses had a septic tank usually underground in the back garden, but the older houses and cottages had changed little in respect of dealing with waste products. Many of these septic tanks probably still exist but the author clearly remembers his being broken and filled in. Some of the concrete lid had been broken and a large chunk was thrown into the void. Next there was a loud 'splodge' sound followed almost immediately by a high arcing fountain of material. It reached a fair height then began its descent to impact all over the person who threw the concrete in. Every piece of his clothing had to be burnt.

1969: Roads Surfaced

Both North Street and West Street had new road surfaces laid, and the footpaths and kerbs were renewed for the whole lengths of each.

1969: Dental Care Film

During April and May a documentary film entitled *Out of the Mouths* concerning dental health was made

Arthur Janes in the doorway of No. 92 near the crossroads, to which he had retired, in about 1967.

Bere Regis church choir on 13 April 1969. Left to right, back row: Pam Collis, Wilfred Harding, Mary Kircher-Smith, Brenda Pitfield, Arthur Yeo, Geoffrey Booth, John England, Perce Mintern, Winifred Mintern, Blanche Coombes, Fred Pitfield, Gladys Smith (organist), Eddie Rawbone; front row: John Pitfield, David Miller, Martin Mullins, John Marsh, Revd Paul Tranter (vicar 1961–76), Mark Pitfield, Donovan Keen, Timothy Maunder, Christopher Booth.

General view of gravel extraction workings on Black Hill in 1969.

Carnival day, July 1965. Left to right, back row: Phyl MacDonald, Jean Percy, Vera Standfield, Stephen MacDonald; middle row: Margaret Tucker, Jack Trim, Jimmy Trim?, ?, Nick MacDonald, Steven Percy; front row: Moira Fripp, Phyl Hopkins, 'Dreamy' Bartlett, ?, Chris Hopkins, Lewis Bartlett. Their float theme was 'Gypsy Encampment'.

Above: *Aerial photograph of Bere Regis dated 18 February 1970.*

Above right: *Winner of the Inter-School Sports held at Broadmayne Primary School in July 1970 was Bere Regis School. Headmaster Mr Stacey is in the centre, with Miss Wood, a supply teacher, at the back.*

Right: *North Street showing Nos 96 to 99. Fred King prepares to cross the road.*

Bere Regis Primary School, Class 5 of 1970. Left to right, back row: Elizabeth Miller, Gregory Jones, Christopher Booth, Steven Ives, Timothy Maunder, Angela Amey, Kevin Hewitt, Leslie Poor, John Pitfield; standing: Robert Presslee, Tina Fancy, Lindsey McLeod, Mark Chambers, Amanda Watts, Beverly Maidment, Steven Ballet, Martin Runyard, Christine Knight, Marion Crocker; seated: Nigel Wright, Barry Rabbits, June Story, Amanda Gough, Sharon Beeden, Eric Gosney (headmaster), Pauline Cook, Marylyn Mitten, Andrew Baker, Graham Pashen. Front row: Christopher Hewitt, Kevin Day, Martin Treviss, Gerald Holloway, Kevin Spicer, Kevin Rolls, Russell Phillips, Mark Bennett, Glyn Bastian, Perry Spicer.

largely in Bere Regis. The film lasted about 25 minutes and was shot mostly at Bere Regis School, but some scenes were shot in Bemister's Stores and on Black Hill. Further scenes were filmed at a PTA social in the Drax Arms music room on the evening of 6 May 1969, and these scenes were used to punctuate the film between footage of the children making the 'Care of Teeth' project in school. The film had a premier in London and was shown to children and parents at the school on Thursday 15 January 1970. A small part of the film was shown on the BBC television programme *Tomorrow's World* on Wednesday 11 February 1970.

1969: Head teacher makes a Splash
Work on the school swimming-pool began in March 1968, worked on by volunteer parents. Site preparation and levelling, then building work took place through the summer of 1968 but work stopped during the winter. The rest of the work, including the footpath, pipework and filter house, were completed during the spring and early summer of 1969.

The grand opening ceremony came on 14 June 1969 following the village carnival and procession up to the school. There were about 20 floats with one themed on the Pool Building Committee itself. The culmination of the pool-opening ceremony was after the speeches when headmaster Alan Stacey was thrown into the pool fully clothed. A villager had filmed some of the day's events on 8mm movie film, which still exists, and captured other carnival and fête events including a swimming relay race, side-shows and table-top games, a piano-smashing event (using sledgehammers!) and all the fun of the fair.

1969: Dealing with Damp Walls
In November work began on repairing the plastering of the walls inside the church. The old plaster was removed, which revealed a bricked-up fireplace in the south aisle. It is almost certainly the fireplace mentioned in the churchwarden's accounts for 1630 and was built so that the Turberville family could keep warm in the winter months. While excavating outside the church's south wall, to reduce damp penetration, a penny dating from 1689–94, the time of King William and Queen Mary was found.

1970: Village Character Dies
Arthur Janes died in January 1970. He had been born in 1884, took over his father's saddlery and harness business, and worked at the shop on the crossroads. In the 1950s he operated two taxis and a cattle-haulage business.

1970: From 2 Miles Up
A vertical aerial photograph was taken of the village on 18 February 1970 from a height of about 10,000ft (3,000m). It covers an area from Bere Heath in the south to Bere Down in the north and Dorchester Hill and Poole Hill in the west and east respectively.

Particular points of interest are the extensive gravel extraction workings on Black Hill, which show up as a huge scar on the top of that heath-covered hill and considerably more hedges in all areas around Bere Regis. The school swimming-pool is clearly visible and it is apparent that the bunching shed at Southbrook covers a large area. Also the large building for the Bere Regis & District Motors bus parking is clearly visible to the west of the church. Boswell's Close is in the last stages of construction as the road has not been paved and appears as a chalk track. Doddings Farm shows up as a particularly active site with many buildings visible. The photo shows the village before many of the developments began that expanded the village just ten years later.

1970: Old masters, New Masters
At Bere Regis Primary School, Mr E.A. Stacey stepped down as headmaster in August at the end of summer term. Between August and December 1970 Mr Peter Malarkey of the County Supply Staff became temporary headmaster. In 1973 there were 133 children on the register. Shortly after this Mr Eric Gosney became headmaster of the Primary School until the end of 1982.

1971: Cress and Farming Firm Splits
Changes at the firm Bedford & Jesty at Bere Regis came in 1971 when Bedford and Jesty divided. William Bedford had died on 20 April 1936, and the firm had already bought a watercress site at Waddock Cross in 1965. In 1971 one half of the business consolidated the Waddock and other sites including Tincleton and Ilsington, with the other half keeping the Bere Regis cress beds.

Developments in the industry during the 1960s had included dealing with a virus that made watercress leaves turn a mosaic yellow, and this was solved by only growing cress from seed. The growing season runs from May to October and typically, from 10,000 seeds sown, 1,000 seedlings are produced, of which only 100 plants grow. The mature beds need 5,000 gallons of pure spring water per acre per hour so that each acre over a growing season requires 22 million gallons of fresh water. The concrete-edged cress beds at Doddings were serviced by a 14-inch-gauge railway which towed the wagons of cress to the bunching house at Southbrook.

1971: Final Use as a Small Shop
Mr R.E. Hogg opened his upholstery shop at No. 82 West Street in 1971. The ground floor was used as his workshop in which he not only repaired furniture but built from new in traditional materials and using traditional methods. His product was of such high quality that it was suggested that Mr Hogg lived in grand circumstances at Milborne St Andrew; something he refuted with a photo of his home stuck on the door which certainly disproved that rumour.

He travelled to work in a vintage car which was always parked outside the shop and drew attention from passers-by. Mr Hogg regularly sat outside the shop working on small parts of the chairs or *chaise longues* and would always talk to people and became one of the village's characters until his retirement in the 1990s, when the shop was converted into a dwelling.

1971: Ex- and Future Premier
Harold Wilson, ex-Prime Minister and leader of the Labour opposition, stopped for lunch at the Royal Oak on 25 July 1971, on his way to the annual Tolpuddle Martyrs Rally. He was the main speaker at the Tolpuddle event during the afternoon after the march through that village. On his way into the pub he was assailed by a throng of children proffering autograph books which he duly signed. Then, about an hour and a half later, Mr and Mrs Wilson re-emerged to be greeted by much the same group of book-waving children and another signing session followed.

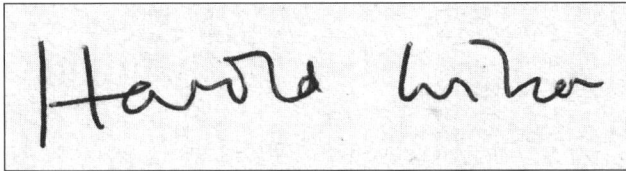

Autograph of Harold Wilson obtained at Bere Regis on 25 July 1971.

Bere Regis under-16 football team after winning the District League Cup in March 1972. Left to right, back row: Len 'Dapper' Hall, Ian 'Jock' McLeod, Steve Painter, Adrian 'Willie' Welstead, Andrew Barter, Russell 'Frew' Hewitt, Robin Hall, Donovan Keen; front row: Ken Davis?, Alan Crocker, Keith Beale, Paul 'Butch' Jeeves, Steve Davis?

1971: Census Figures
Village population from the census is 1,235.

1973: Post Office Changes
After about three weeks of conversion work, No. 84

West Street opened as the new Post Office on Monday 29 October 1973. The new postmaster was Major Knowler. The previous Post Office at No. 13 North Street had closed on Saturday 27 October 1973 where Mrs Munroe had carried on the duties as postmistress since the death of her husband Major J. Munroe.

1975: Restoration Celebrations
There was a celebration of the Restoration of the Church on 2 October 1975 to commemorate 100 years since the reopening. One of the events in the church was a play performed by children of the village primary school, in which two children travelled back in time with a model of Dr Who's Tardis and explained what they could see around them during a trip of 1,000 years. The time-travel trip ended in the present after their penultimate stop had been in 1875, during the restoration work. The week-long celebrations concluded on 4 October 1975 with a firework display on Court Green.

1976: Striking Summer of '76
The summer of 1975 had been the best for many years but was eclipsed by the summer of '76, which is still cited today for its heat and long dry period. The high temperatures began in May, continued through June culminating in a temperature in the vicarage garden of 108°F (42.2°C) on 27 June 1976. There was no rain and by July the stream had dried up completely. It was a popular walk from Shitterton Bridge all along the dried river bed to return to the hot pavements of Southbrook bridge without getting one's feet wet. The surrounding fields, normally green at this time of year, prematurely turned first golden then a dirty brown and the fire risks were huge; the heathland on the slopes of Black Hill caught fire on several occasions. Emergency water-supplies were provided for the cattle on the farms of the village.

August and the beginning of September continued with similar temperatures but thunderstorms and heavy rain through September brought the heat wave to an end in dramatic fashion. The south-west pinnacle of the church was struck by lightning on 25 September 1976 dislodging it to fall over 60ft to impact in pieces next to the base of the tower.

1976: New Bere Regis Vicar
Revd Dennis Shaw was instituted vicar of Bere Regis on 3 December 1976. He resigned in May 1985.

1978: Balloon Passes Over
Double Eagle II, nearing the end of the first hot-air balloon flight across the Atlantic, drifted directly above Bere Regis at 11a.m. on 17 August 1978. Its three Americans from Presque Island, Maine, were making headline news, having reached off-shore Europe and looking set to go further. Having been brought to Britain by the jet stream, and still high in the sky, a north-westerly wind continued to carry

On the corner of West Street and Butt Lane the 65 foot long ex-First World War hut which was converted to two dwellings called The Laurels. This photo is dated 24 December 1979.

White Lovington was a new estate of houses built in the 1980s replacing White Lovington House.

The crossroads at Bere Regis on 1 January 1979.

Chalk excavation, using heavy machinery, for the bypass on 11 August 1981.

Excavation of chalk at the bypass workings in April 1981.

them towards Poole Harbour and the English Channel. They made their landfall south-east of Paris, which brought the historic adventure to a close after 5 days, 17 hours, 6 minutes in the air, and a distance of 3,150 miles. The crewmen were Ben Abruzzo, Maxie Anderson and Larry Newman.

1980: Parish Magazine Editor
Between July 1980 and April 1981 the editor of the Bere Regis section of the parish magazine was Simon Regan (1942–2000). Mr Regan, who was born in Weymouth, had been a campaigning journalist for many years starting at the *News Of The World* in 1968 after moving to London. He left after the publication of his book, a biography of Rupert Murdoch. The book was reviewed in *The Times* and was described as 'disgracefully ill-written and ill-constructed'.

Mr Regan's editorship of the parish magazine in those seven months added a cosmopolitan colour all his own. Journalist in-jokes and tirades against the youth of Bere Regis resulted in him being pelted with eggs on one occasion, not to mention the letting down of his car tyres more than once. He had successfully created the very situation he was protesting about.

Simon Regan was about to rise to the full heights of journalistic pride when he appeared on the front pages of all the newspapers on 6 May 1981. During the royal tour of Australia, taped conversations between Prince Charles and Lady Diana Spencer were leaked to Regan and he sold them to the press. Regan moved away from the village and later continued publishing books on the royal family until 1989, when he began producing a magazine from Dorset

Left: *Glass bottle found in a tunnel under Court Green Farm in August 1981.*

Left: *Tarmacking the final surface at the back of Barrow Hill, for Bere Regis bypass, pictured on 10 May 1982.*

Work proceeding on the bypass at Bere Regis where the Milborne road crosses beneath, 13 March 1982.

Bere Regis bypass opening ceremony on 5 July 1982 ended with the ribbon cutting by Minister of Transport Lynda Chalker MP. Local MP Lord Cranborne is on the left.

called *Scallywag*. Legal action followed his articles on what he perceived were Dorset-based scandals. *Scallywag* reached issue number 13 before being closed down after action resulting from accusations regarding Prime Minister John Major. The issue sold 115,000 copies.

1981: Bypass for Bere Regis
Work began on the Bere Regis bypass in 1981. By the end of January 1981 posts were set out across the fields from Dorchester Hill, around Town's End Farm and across to the Poole road. Test bore holes were drilled after this to find the exact depth of topsoil. During February the posts were replaced with the fence (still in place) which marked the boundary of the workings.

The process of removing the topsoil began in March 1981, while electrical poles and pylons that crossed the workings were raised to allow the passage of heavy machinery. The small haunted (or so we had been told) wood at the end of Chalkey Lane was levelled and the trees burned on 13 March. By the end of March the place where the little wood had been was being scraped and lowered to fit the final shape of the landscape west of where the filling station is situated.

During June and July 1981 the excavations continued to be made deeper and deeper. The final level when measured at the point where Butt Lane crossed was 15ft (5m) below the level of the old lane. The deepest point of the road level, where the road cut through the back of Barrow Hill, is situated is 82ft (25m) below the previous level.

In August topsoil started to be placed on the slopes of the cuttings and the underpass for the road to Roke was being completed and covered with topsoil. Both roundabouts for the A31 and A35 respectively were being worked on with vehicles on these roads being diverted and controlled by temporary traffic lights. The road along the top of the Recreation Ground was brought up to its present level. Crushed limestone ballast was added around the Town's End area during September and tarmacking began from the Dorchester Hill end.

Tidying up all aspects of the excavations continued through the early winter of 1981. The winter and spring of 1982 involved the continuation of surfacing from the Dorchester Hill end to the two roundabouts and landscaping after the adjustment of the various levels, and by early summer 1982 it was finished. The contractors had been MacAlpine and the official opening ceremony was on 5 July 1982. Brief speeches were made from an improvised podium and the ribbon was cut by Minister of Transport, Lynda Chalker MP.

1981: Population Census
The population of the village in this year was recorded at 1,427.

1981: Cricket Renaissance
As a result of an off-the-cuff challenge during the course of a session in the Royal Oak there was a friendly cricket match between regulars at the Oak and an improvised team of farmers from the village. The match took place at Winterborne Kingston Cricket Club and was enjoyed so much that a revival was inevitable after that May 1981 match.

1982: Cricket Re-formed
In March Bere Regis Cricket Club was re-formed in the dining-room of the Royal Oak pub. Affiliation with Bere Regis Sports Club followed and fund-raising events included a sponsored walk to the Silent Woman pub for lunch, to Bloxworth for tea, and back to Bere through Bere Wood. There was also a clay-pigeon shoot at Bere Heath Farm organised by Jim Shave of Rye Hill Farm ending with a demonstration of shooting with a 4-bore gun by Geoff Orchard. The Cricket Club was built up over the following year such that League Cricket was being played in 1983 and the new clubhouse was opened in 1984. This replaced the 1960-vintage pavilion to the west of the pitch. The clubhouse was converted from the stone barn formerly attached to Townsend Farm, since moved up Cow Drove towards Woodbury Hill.

1983: Annual Fireworks
A random invitation to teacher Claire Truswell in November 1982 resulted in her having the idea to have village firework displays at the school to raise funds. The party she had been invited to was for a private firework display in Butt Lane where she also lived. The first event was in November 1983 and since then the school has hosted an event each year. Weather and financial depression makes the event variable but numbers reached 1,000 at least twice.

The 400th anniversary of Guy Fawkes's capture and his treasonous gunpowder plot was celebrated on 5 November 2005.

1983: All Change in the Village
An aerial photograph of Bere Regis was taken on 19 August 1983 from an altitude of about 1,500ft (460m). It shows the Methodist chapel still standing and the many buildings of the new estate in place, including Turberville Court. The adjacent buildings of the firm G. & L. Barnes are evident but the site opposite where Cyril Wood Court is now located, can be seen as gardens and a lawn adjacent to the road. Less than a year after the new bypass opened the altered roads are clearly visible.

1983: New Headmaster
At Bere Regis Primary School Mr Charles Innes took over as headmaster. He held the position until 1990, although Miss Claire Truswell was the acting headmistress from the autumn term 1988 until summer term 1989.

Scale model of Bere Regis Coaches bus at the Dorchester office in 1984.

1984: Surgery and Clinic

The new surgery and clinic opened on Monday 8 October 1984 on the corner of Manor Farm Road and Turberville Road in Bere Regis. The previous surgery at Broadwater on Roke Road closed permanently on Friday 5 October. Dr P.J.D. Benjafield had retired from the Dorset Medical List on 30 April 1984 but the surgery remained functioning at his home until the new clinic was completed, with Dr Greenfield being granted partnership succession. The new partner is Dr T.G. Harley.

1985: New Vicar for Bere

The Revd Jonathan Burke is instituted vicar of Bere Regis on 24 June 1985, and resigned on 9 June 1992.

Left: *Revd Jonathan Burke was vicar of Bere Regis from 1985 to 1992. He is pictured on duty at a stall at the 14 July 1990 carnival.*

Revd Dennis Shaw (right) *hands over to Revd Jonathon Burke in 1985.*

1986: Bus Firm Changes

The government deregulated the operation of private bus companies in Britain and, with its 83-vehicle fleet of coaches, Bere Regis & District Motor Services adapted its routes and services. In June 1983 they had started a Dorset to London service competing directly with the rail service from Wool or Wareham. The firm had depots at Bere Regis, Dorchester, Blandford, Hazelbury Bryan, Sherborne, Wimborne and Weymouth. The importance of private hire, holiday tours and contract work began to replace the timetabled network. Typical of these changes was the introduction of a town service in Dorchester started in 1989 and big contract work for British Petroleum to transport workers to the Wytch oilfield in Purbeck, which at full capacity involved 25 coaches. The three main partners in the firm had all passed away by this time; Percy Davis in 1964, Bill Ironside in 1970 and Reg Toop in 1973.

1987: White Lovington

White Lovington House was demolished by August 1987 and a development begun for 16 detached houses built during the next couple of years. The land used was that occupied by the original house and a wooded area around the house which had almost completely obscured the building for about 60 years. The development is called White Lovington.

West Street looking east near Shitterton. The 65ft-long ex-First World War hut is seen in June 1986. The east end of the hut had been a house for the staff of West End Garage.

Rye Hill Close, just before the slope of Rye Hill begins, was built in about 1989.

The Methodist chapel, pictured on 30 June 1986 from the car park.

Cyril Wood Court workroom behind the function room, as pictured in May 1994.

View from the church tower on 7 July 1994 looking north. Cyril Wood Court complex is visible in the middle distance.

View from the church tower looking west, 24 June 1989. Turberville Court is in the foreground and there are two Bere Regis coaches in the car park.

Right: *The Scout Hut was completed and opened in 1989.*

Below: *The carnival on 20 July 1991, here being led up West Street by the Wareham Town Band.*

1987: Methodist Chapel Goes
The Methodist chapel, which had been used as a builder's firm workshop since 1962, was demolished by 19 September 1987

1987: The Great Gale
On the night of 15–16 October 1987 the remains of a real hurricane swept across the south of England. Damage in Bere Regis included many trees being felled and a 10,000-volt power line being blown down to the south of the village. Emergency services were employed to make that situation safe. Minor structural damage was widespread but the road to Wareham through Bere Wood and Wareham Forest was blocked at several places by fallen trees. Nationally on that night there were 18 deaths and the 100m.p.h. winds brought down 15 million trees.

1989: Rye Hill Close
In about this year, Rye Hill Close was built. It consists of five houses and three semi-detached houses between the road from Southbrook to the school at Rye Hill, and on the east side stretches across to the river. There had been a large thatched barn next to the road where the entrance now is, but this was pulled down in 1972.

1989: Turberville Descendants
The ascendancy of the internet brought about an almost Hardyesque revival of the Turberville name. It was found to be alive and well in the United States, with Mrs Joan T. Westmoreland claiming direct descent in Palmetto, Georgia, and Bryan R. Turbeville [sic] living in Birmingham, Alabama.

1989: Elder Road Scout Hut
The new Scout Hut was officially opened on 27 September 1989 by Admiral John Croydon, the Dorset County Commissioner for Scouts. Building work had begun in 1986 by volunteers and members at a site west of the Southbrook cress beds with an entrance on Elder Road. Up until this time the Bere Regis Scouts had shared the ex-First World War hut with the Women's Institute at Southbrook.

1990: New Headmaster
Bere Regis Primary School appoints a new headmaster, Mr Steven Battishill.

1991: Village Developments
An aerial photograph of Bere Regis was taken on 13 January from a height of about 2,000ft (600m) and looking north from a position above Black Hill. It not only shows the completed estate part of the village between West Street and the river, but the completion of new housing to the west toward Shitterton. The industrial units area near the roundabout joining the A31 road have been built but work had not started on the new filling station. The new housing development at White Lovington looks almost complete.

Above: *Harvesting on Bere Down, 31 August 1991.*

Right: *Cricket at the Recreation Ground on 17 August 1991. Bere Regis are fighting back with 54 for 2 against the Old Blandfordians team.*

1991: Census Figures
Village population from the census was 1,767.

1992: Seven Sleeping Policemen
Seven traffic-calming 'humps' were built through the village – in West Street between the Royal Oak and West Mill. The work was finished by September 1992.

1993: Military Vicar for Bere
The Ven. Graham Roblin is instituted as vicar of Bere Regis (and Affpuddle) on 16 January 1993. Mr Roblin was the former army chaplain and deputy chaplain general to the armed forces and archdeacon of the army based at Bagshot Park in Surrey. Originally from Cardiff he had been chaplain for 26 years after serving as a curate in South London. He was educated at Exeter Cathedral Choir School and King's College, Taunton. During his time as army chaplain he served in Germany, the Far East and Northern Ireland. Mr Roblin retired on 7 October 2001.

View from the top of the siren tower at the fire station, on 4 August 1994.

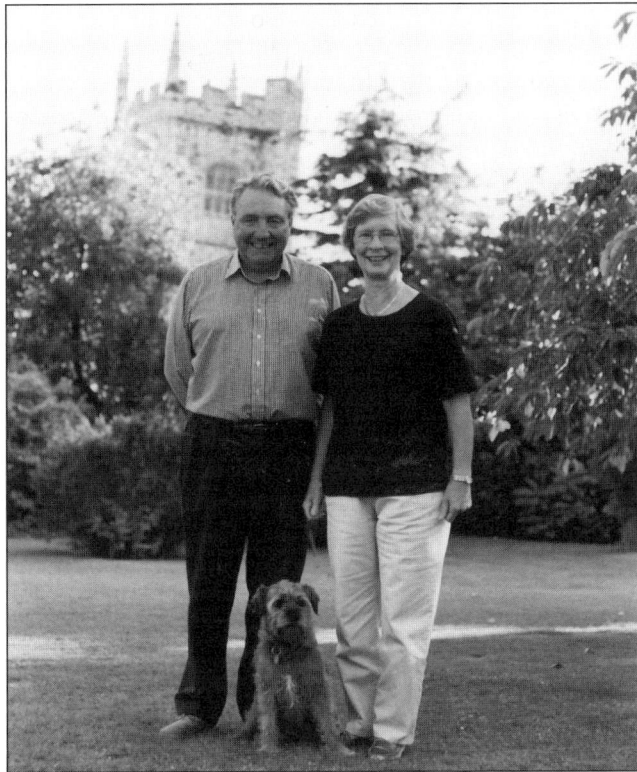

The Ven. Graham Roblin and wife Penelope in the vicarage garden in August 2001. Muffett the dog is loyally in attendance.

1995: Bere Regis & District Name Ceases
The name of Bere Regis & District Motor Services ceased after the closure of the offices at Blandford and Wimborne. These two sites were all that remained of the business after 1994 when most of the routes and services and the Dorchester base were sold to Dorchester Coachways and West Dorset Coaches.

Between 1994 and the closure, a small number of private hire vehicles carried on the Bere Regis name

and livery with garages in Wimborne, controlled from an office in Blandford. The head office of the Bere Regis firm, at Bridport Road in Dorchester, was finally closed in April 2001, although then under the coaching name First Dorchester.

1997: Urn Found at Barrow Hill
A Romano-British (first–fourth century) burial urn, with bones, was found during a soak pit excavation on the slopes of Barrow Hill on the Butt Lane side. The urn was about 5ins high and 6ins wide.

1999: Church Illumination
At 6.00p.m. on the eve of the new millennium new floodlights in the churchyard were switched on for the first time to illuminate the church from all sides. There had been a small number of lights around the church for many years, but this complete lighting system was given in memory of the Revd Roland Charles Herring and his wife Margaret. Mr Herring was vicar of Bere Regis from 1936 until 1960.

2002: New Vicar of Bere Regis
The Revd Ian Woodward was inducted as vicar of Bere Regis on 23 January 2002.

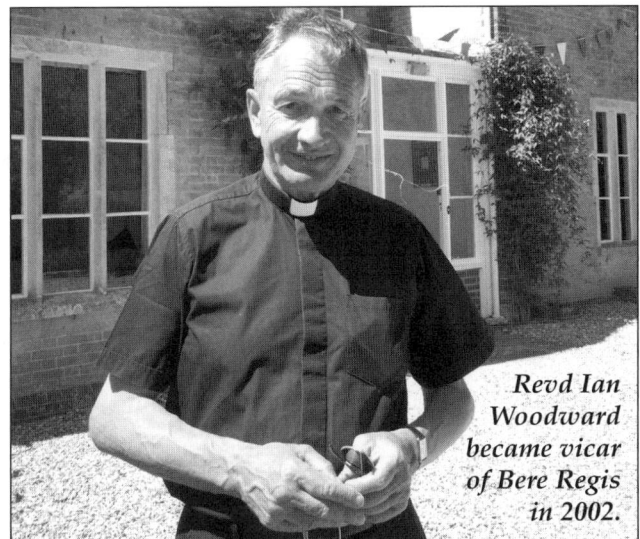

Revd Ian Woodward became vicar of Bere Regis in 2002.

2003: Court Green Unveiled

In December 2003 and January 2004 Bournemouth University Archaeology students did a resistivity survey of Court Green field. They found some of the old Manor House, underground tunnels, walls, and other buildings.

2005: The Dominant Car

A road traffic survey was conducted in the village part of Bere Regis at Sunday lunchtime on 6 March 2005. The count was of parked cars and vans visible from the highway and included garages that were obviously in use. There were 158 on the 1980s-built estate part of the village and 82 on West Street. The other streets were: Shitterton (59), South Mead (39), Butt Lane (28), Back Lane (10), Snow Hill & Boswell's Close (63), North Street (45), Royal Oak to Rye Hill (68), Egdon Close (47), Rye Hill Close (26), White Lovington (8), Green Close (44) and Surgery to Turberville Court (45). The number of vehicles totalled 722, while for the whole parish an estimate of 900–1,000 was predicted.

2006: Neolithic Flint Tool Found

In April 2006 a flint shard worked and knapped to form a Neolithic multi-use borer and scraper was found on the slopes of Barrow Hill, on the Butt Lane side. It is about 2ins (50mm) long and 1.5in (38mm) wide. It probably pre-dates the Bronze Age barrow at Barrow Hill, by at least 1,000 years (i.e. 3500BC).

Found in April 2006, this Neolithic-flint boring tool could also be used as a scraper.

Bere Regis church garden party, 24 June 2006.

Aerial Pictures:
Bere From the Sky, 2006

The following pages show aerial views of Bere Regis. All photographs were taken on 12 April 2006.

Subscribers

Robert J. Abbott, Bere Regis

Roger Angel and Judy Newton, Bere Regis, Dorset

Mr and Mrs G.L. Baker, Goodwood, Australia

Clifford L. and Jean M. Barnes, Bere Regis, Dorset

David J.D. Barnes, Poole, Dorset

Mrs Doris A. Barnes, Bere Regis

Mr Martin J. Bartlett, Bere Regis, Dorset

Lewis and Margaret Bartlett, Bere Regis, Dorset

Amy Bennett, Bere Regis

Cyril Bennett, Bere Regis, Dorset

Mark and Diana Bennett, Bere Regis, Dorset

Paul and Alison Bennett, Bere Regis

Tom Bennett, Bere Regis

Robin C. Bloomfield C.B.E., Chamberlaynes Farm, Bere Regis

G.E. Bower, Sandford, Nr Wareham, Dorset

Betty and Harry Brown, Shitterton, Bere Regis

Peg Browning, Brockhill

Cythya Burden, Bere Regis

Mr and Mrs Edward and Lorraine Butterfield, Bere Regis

Cérences, Normandie, Twinned with Bere Regis, Dorset

Mary Chamberlain, Bere Regis, Dorset

Pat Chesney, Bere Regis

Gordon L. Cleall, Bere Regis, Dorset

William F. Cleall, Bere Regis, Dorset

John and Rosemary Cleave, Bere Regis, Dorset

Lesley A. Clinch, Poole, Dorset

Tom and Angela Crabtree, Bere Regis

Mr Ian Cuff

Margaret L. Dann, Bere Regis, Dorset

Alison and Martin Debenham, Shitterton

Ruth and Anthony Draycott, Bere Regis, Dorset

Roger and Arlene Duncanson, Bere Regis, Dorset

Wally Dyke, Bere Regis, Dorset

David Eastment, Blandford, Dorset

John Eastment, Moreton, Dorset

Michael Eastment, Bere Regis, Dorset

Mr Peter Elford, Bere Regis, Dorset

Mrs Susan Evans, Bere Regis

L.W. Fairhurst, Bere Regis, Dorset

Patricia A. Fancy, Bere Regis, Dorset

Brenda Farwell and Hugh Gibson, Bere Regis, Dorset

Mary and Roy Farwell, Bere Regis, Dorset

M.T. and K. Furlong, Bere Regis, Dorset

B. Gale, Bere Regis, Dorset

Guy and Ginny Glanville, Bere Regis, Dorset

Mr and Mrs C.R. Goddard, Bere Regis

Douglas Gould, North Street, Bere Regis

George and Gwyneth Hall, Kinson, Bournemouth

Jonathan D. Hart, Bere Regis, Dorset

David D. Herring, Bere Regis

Alan, Mandy and Glen Hewitt, Bere Regis, Dorset

Cyril B. Hewitt

Anthony House, Bere Regis

Mr and Mrs R. Howe, Blandford Forum, Dorset

G.T. Ireland, Bere Down Farm, Bere Regis

Bob and Sue James, Bere Regis, Dorset

Bob and Gill Jennings, Bere Regis, Dorset

Jolyon Jesty, Long Island, USA

Pauline Jesty, Bere Regis, Dorset

S. and A. Jolliffe, Bere Regis, Dorset

Raymond and Angela Jones, Bere Regis, Dorset

Robin D. Kinahan

Des Lambert, Hamworthy, Dorset
I.M. Lennox-Gordon
Garry Lewis, Bere Regis
Mary and Leslie Lewis, Bere Regis
Julien and Bernadette Lightfoot
Mr and Mrs Alec Lillie, Bere Regis, Dorset
The Lloyd Family, Bere Regis, Dorset
Robin P. Lockyer, Poole, Dorset
P. and P. Lockyer, Dorchester, Dorset
Eileen G. Maidment, Bere Regis, Dorset
Ron Margetts, Bere Regis, Dorset
Ann Osborne (née Percy), Dorchester, Dorset
Stephen Percy, Bere Regis, Dorset
James E. Percy, Bere Regis, Dorset
Gorden L. Phillips, Bere Regis, Dorset
Michael and Sharon Pipe, Bere Regis, Dorset
John and Bronwen Pitman, Geenayr, Bere Regis
Martin R. Pitman, Dorchester, Dorset
Mr W.R. Pitman and Mrs S.E. Pitman (née Hewitt), Bere Regis, Dorset
Michael Presslee, Dorchester, Dorset
Janice Reeves, Green Close, Bere Regis
Ronald Ricketts, Tolpuddle, Dorset
Eileen Salisbury, Bere Regis, Dorset
Leonard and Susan Skinner, Bere Regis
Mr J. and Mrs D. Smith, Bere Regis, Dorset

Michael J. Standfield, Southbrook, Bere Regis
Lisa Standfield, Chamberlaynes, Bere Regis
Ken Stickley, Bere Regis, Dorset
Donald and Wendy Thorne, Chamberlaynes, Bere Regis
Charles and Debbie Tibbey, Bere Regis, Dorset
Pauline Townson, Shitterton, Bere Regis
Mr Walter S.K. Trim, Bere Regis, Dorset
Christine Tucker, Bere Regis, Dorset
Ian and Diana Ventham, Shitterton
Mrs Claire L. Waite, Bere Regis, Dorset
Dr Simon and Mrs Tina Walker, North Street, Bere Regis
John F.W. Walling, Newton Abbot, Devon
Eddie and Margaret Watkins, Bere Heath
Elizabeth M. Watkins, Bere Heath, Bere Regis, Dorset
Patricia M. Watkins, Bere Heath, Bere Regis, Dorset
Eric Westropp, Bloxworth, Dorset
Richard and Tina White, Bere Regis, Dorset
Mr C.A. White, 'Leawood', Bloxworth, Dorset
Arthur Thomas Whitty I.S.M.,
Rosemary Wise, Bere Regis, Dorset
John and Margaret Wrixon, Bere Regis

❖